900 YEARS:
THE RESTORATIONS OF
WESTMINSTER ABBEY

*This Catalogue is published on the occasion of
the Exhibition in St Margaret's Church, Westminster
and the Masons' Yard, Westminster Abbey,
May to September 1995*

900 YEARS:
THE RESTORATIONS OF
WESTMINSTER ABBEY

by Thomas Cocke

with contributions by Donald Buttress
Surveyor of the Fabric of Westminster Abbey

Foreword by

The Prince Philip, Duke of Edinburgh, KG, KT

Published for

THE DEAN & CHAPTER OF WESTMINSTER
by HARVEY MILLER PUBLISHERS

Originating Publisher:
HARVEY MILLER PUBLISHERS
Knightsbridge House, 197 Knightsbridge, London SW7 lRB

An Imprint of G + B Arts International

British Library in Publication Data
A catalogue record for this book is available
from the British Library

Hardback: ISBN 1-872501-77-X
Paperback: ISBN 1-872501-82-6

Printed and bound by
BAS Printers Ltd
Over Wallop, Stockbridge, Hampshire
Manufactured in Great Britain

Contents

A colour-coded plan of Westminster Abbey (Westlake, 1923) faces page 9

Work on the restoration of the exterior of the Abbey started in 1973 and now, twenty two years, an economic recession and twenty five million pounds later, the most extensive restoration carried out since at least the time of Sir Christopher Wren, has been completed; although, needless to say, the work of routine maintenance continues as ever. None of this would have been possible without the support of many hundreds of generous and long-suffering donors.

The skills of today's craftsmen, as can be seen at first hand in this exhibition, are fully up to the standards of their predecessors and there is the same combination of respect for the design and purpose of the original with imaginative touches of contemporary detail and style. The dedication of all involved in the process of restoration has been quite outstanding.

This scholarly and beautifully illustrated catalogue tells the story of the evolution of the present Abbey through conservation, re-building, restoration and repair ever since the first building on the site was dedicated by Edward the Confessor, its founder, on 28 December 1065.

I hope that everyone for whom the Abbey is a place of unique religious, historical and architectural interest will find this catalogue and exhibition worthy of a building which is held in such affection by so many people in this country, the Commonwealth and the world.

I. Westminster Abbey, West Front

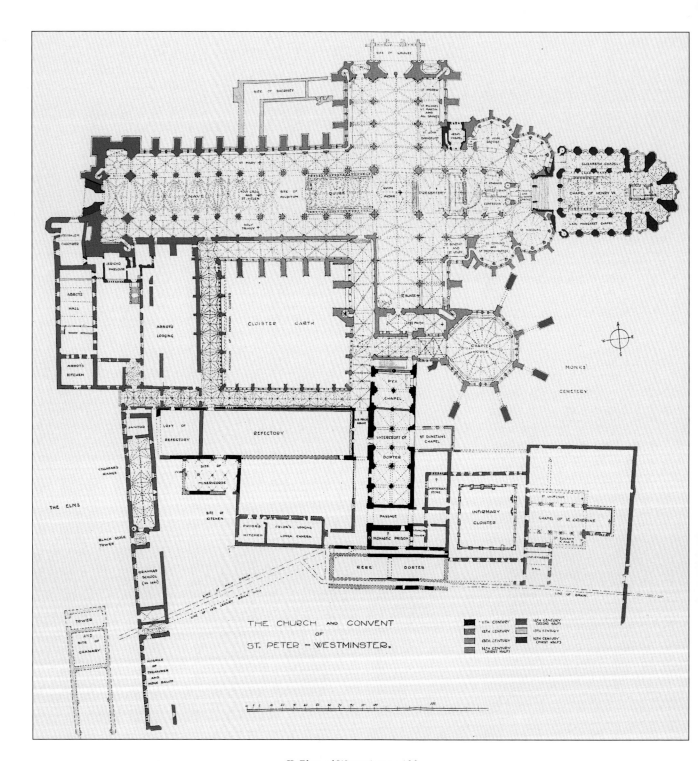

II. Plan of Westminster Abbey

Preface

THIS CATALOGUE describes and illustrates how Westminster Abbey has been transformed over the past nine centuries. Both its structure and its contents have been changed and changed about, but the identity of the building has never been lost. This process of change deserves chronicling as a subject in its own right, not as an apologetic footnote explaining why certain original features have been modified. For those of the Gothic Revival such as William Morris, even by the 1890s the exterior of the Abbey had been 'damaged so vitally...that we have nothing left us but a mere outline, a ghost.'[1] The 'ghost' has proved remarkably robust, the latest century of its history encompassing both aerial attack and painstaking restoration. This is a story worth telling.

Restoration, according to the meaning we give it today as a self-conscious process of repair and reinstatement of earlier features, only came to the Abbey at the end of the seventeenth century, with the campaign of comprehensive repair devised and carried out by Christopher Wren and his successors. This programme of work, covering the entire building both inside and out and setting out deliberately to respect the style of the original structure, was exceptional for its date, not only in England but anywhere in Europe.

Restoration can also be used in a wider sense to cover a process of renovation whereby the original fabric is replaced to a different design and in a different style but respecting the meaning and ethos of the building. A famous example was the replacement by Bramante of the Early Christian basilica of St Peter's in Rome with his Renaissance design, not regarded then as an act of vandalism, but as a restatement of the significance of the building for a new age. The continuing vitality of an institution can be said to be expressed better by refashioning its buildings in a fresh style, rather than by patching up the old. It is in this way that the replacement of the Confessor's Romanesque abbey church by Henry III in the up-to-date Gothic style can be considered as a work of restoration, not as a new building.

The meaning of restoration at Westminster can be vividly illustrated by a topical example: the history of the effigy of Queen Elizabeth I, as revealed in the recent programme of conservation.[2] This figure was dismissed for years as a second-rate eighteenth-century copy of the original. Indeed the exterior of the Abbey has been regarded in a similar way. However, in the effigy as in the building, not only is the eighteenth-century interpretation of the earlier period important in its own right, but the early fabric turns out to remain at the heart. The effigy acquired a new head and new clothes in 1760, not through insensitive vandalism, but to show off

Elizabeth's central role in the Abbey's history more effectively, just as Wren and Hawksmoor had refaced the fabric of the building a few decades before. To try to strip away the contribution of later generations in order to reveal some mythical prime original is a profound misunderstanding of Westminster's rich complexity.

A detailed story of Westminster Abbey's 900 years would require a long series of exhibition halls. To illustrate, in the narrow space available, a chronological overview of the different functions performed by the Abbey throughout the centuries and the different periods of art and forms of religion contained within its walls, we have chosen to conjure up a variety of objects and images. Carved stonework from the twelfth century is juxtaposed with a parchment charter of the sixteenth century and a seventeenth-century velvet cope. Models or detached fragments of architecture and tombs must take the place of the original masterpieces which form integral parts of the Abbey and cannot therefore be moved. Topographical watercolours, architectural drawings, even long-lost sculpted angels fill the gaps in a story where schemes were proposed but abandoned, such as Wren's central steeple, and where objects as large as the Baroque altarpiece were dismantled and dispersed. Sadly, there is no space to examine properly the buildings associated with the Abbey, whether as part of the monastery or of Westminster School. Neither can I do more than note here the importance of the architectural history of St Margaret's Church, which houses the exhibition. The intimate links between St Margaret's and the Houses of Parliament make the restorations of the church particularly significant.

The relationship between the historical overview depicted in St Margaret's and the work in progress seen in the Masons' Yard is vital to the exhibition. The two parts give meaning to each other: the historical context gives validity to the current works, showing how this process of organic renewal has been present at the Abbey from the start, while the display of work in progress brings vividly to life the physical reality of the works exhibited in St Margaret's.

The Abbey's Building History: A Summary

The Romanesque Church

Begun *c.* 1045 by Edward the Confessor following Norman models such as the Abbey of Jumièges outside Rouen, the church was consecrated in 1065 but completed over the following decades. The plan consisted of an apsed sanctuary, transepts, a long nave and a West Front with twin towers. No part of the fabric of the Confessor's church is now visible, although the core of the West Towers is still Romanesque. Work of the period does survive, however, in the former monastic buildings.

Henry III's Church

A Lady Chapel was added to the east of the Romanesque church after 1220 by Abbot William de Humez and may have been similar in style to the Lady Chapel of Salisbury Cathedral or the choir of the Temple Church in London. Henry III began a total reconstruction of the church in 1245 and pursued it as a royal programme until his death in 1272. The plan included a polygonal East End with four polygonal radiating chapels and, on axis, the Lady Chapel, adapted to fit. The crossing was designed as a stage for coronations with deep aisled transepts, that on the south over-arching the cloister. Only five bays of the nave were finished by the time of the king's death. The style of Henry III's church and its proportions were much indebted to French buildings such as the cathedrals of Rheims or Amiens, but it was by no means a copy. There was extravagant use of sculpture and ornament, particularly on the North Transept, and of elaborate furnishings, notably in the Confessor's Shrine. The floors of the Sanctuary and around the Shrine and Henry's tomb were in Cosmatesque mosaic work, derived from Rome.

Later Middle Ages

The nave of the Romanesque church survived in use until 1376 when its rebuilding began. The design of the West Front was settled by *c.* 1400; but the construction of the upper parts of the church took a century. The western towers were not finished by the time the Dissolution halted the work. The style generally conforms with that of Henry III's building, but the more up-to-date Perpendicular style was employed on the West Front. Major changes were introduced inside the church, notably the construction of Henry V's Chantry to the east of the Confessor's Shrine and of a solid altar screen to the west of it.

The Henry VII Chapel

In 1503, King Henry VII rebuilt the thirteenth-century Lady Chapel as a burial place for himself and for his uncle, Henry VI, whom it was hoped would be canonized. It forms a distinct church in itself, with a nave, aisles and a polygonal apse. The style is a rich and bold Perpendicular, developing features in contemporary buildings, notably at Windsor. The pendant fan vault is one of the most remarkable examples of its type in Europe. The furnishings from this period remain largely intact, especially the array of figure sculpture and the bronze Renaissance tombs of Henry VII and his Queen Elizabeth.

Major Restorations

(1) 1699–1745 Comprehensive restoration of the entire fabric of the church, excluding the Henry VII Chapel.
Reconstruction of the lantern and the North Front.

(2) 1809–22 Restoration of the Henry VII Chapel.

(3) 1866–90 Restoration of the Chapter House and the North Transept.

(4) *c.* 1960–95 Restoration and cleaning of the entire Abbey, beginning with the Sanctuary and concluding with the West Towers and the Henry VII Chapel.

I · The Medieval Abbey

Romanesque Beginnings

THE BUILDING of the Romanesque church in the mid eleventh century by Edward the Confessor (1042–66) was a further development of a site which already possessed centuries of history. There is evidence of Roman occupation of the site, in particular a sarcophagus excavated in the nineteenth century between the North Transept and St Margaret's. Yet tradition has it that the history of the Abbey began in early Saxon times. Chronicles and documents surviving from the Middle Ages describe the foundation of the church in the first years of the seventh century by a citizen of London, or perhaps King Sebert of the East Saxons, with the aid of Bishop Mellitus of London, and its miraculous consecration by St Peter himself. Gifts and support recorded from King Offa in the late seventh century and from Archbishop Dunstan in the mid tenth century established a continuous line of ancestry for the later institution. Careful research from the eighteenth century to the present day has exposed the many inaccuracies within this traditional story but has not succeeded in providing an authoritative alternative. Opinions remain divided between those who, at one extreme, regard the Abbey as a seventh-century foundation established as the West-Minster and dedicated to St Peter at the same time as or even before the East-Minster (the Cathedral of St Paul in the old Roman City of London), and those at the other extreme who consider that the Abbey was, until the Confessor's time, a minor community with few valid links with St Dunstan and King Edgar in the tenth century, let alone with more remote patrons. A recent authority concluded that 'it is likely that the first church at Westminster was a Minster Church, dating from the early eighth century and serving an area stretching as far north as present-day Oxford Street.'[1] She would also accept the year 959 as 'the probable date' for St Dunstan's foundation of a Benedictine community at Westminster.[2]

Whatever the truth of these stories, they demonstrate that, even at the time of the consecration of the Confessor's church in 1065, Westminster Abbey already had a context. Although the structure and the design of the building were new, they were shaped by the existing associations of the site. Hence, from the very beginning, one key element of the concept of restoration—the loyalty to an established identity— was already present.

If we wish to conjure up a picture of the abbey church erected by Edward the Confessor, the best way to do so is by studying the present building, not focusing

1. Westminster Abbey in the late eleventh century. Reconstruction drawing by Terry Ball

on the stylistic detail but looking through half-closed eyes at the mass of the design. The topography of river, palace, and church is recognizably the same, as is the contrast between the accessible areas to the north and west and the private areas to the south. The cruciform plan still has a relatively short east arm to house the Sanctuary and a choir extending westwards over the crossing into the long nave, which is terminated by twin western towers. Above all, the Romanesque church established the monumental scale of the building. Although the level site has never allowed Westminster to dominate the landscape like Lincoln or Durham, and although tall modern buildings now compete with it, the Abbey still maintains the complex but majestic bulk that so impressed the author of the near-contemporary *Vita Aedwardi* and probably led him to refer to the 'complex variety of such an immense work' (*multiplicitas tam vasti operis*).[4]

One can also recognize, from the beginning, the wider influences that shaped the Romanesque building, and that still affect the Abbey today. It was royal, not because its construction was funded by a casual act of royal munificence, but because its foundation was sustained by the particular and continuing care of King Edward. This status was immediately marked by two important events, the burial of the Confessor in January 1066 and the Coronation of William the Conqueror on Christmas Day of that same year. These events established the royal associations of the Abbey for future generations. Succeeding monarchs might conduct ceremonial crown-wearings in other cities such as Winchester, and might choose to be buried in other great churches, but a pattern at Westminster as both coronation church and royal mausoleum had been marked out and would indeed be fully developed later. More important, the church was served by a well-endowed monastic community maintaining a continuous round of worship which could respond both to grand national events, such as the Confessor's burial and the Conqueror's Coronation, and to the requirements of the Benedictine Rule to observe a daily sequence of offices and masses. Whatever the changes of later centuries, these characteristic features of Abbey life, the corporate body—whether Monastery, Chapter or College—and its provision of worship, both for the daily round and for special occasions, have never been forgotten.

The Abbey's architectural history during the next two centuries is unclear. It is not known how much of the church was complete at the time of its consecration on 27 December 1065 or whether, if there was a break in construction, the western parts of the building were continued according to the same design or a revised version.[5] Recent analysis of surviving Romanesque fabric incorporated within the present West Towers suggests that the original towers were not erected until well into the twelfth century.[6] The monastery experienced reverses as well as successes, and was

2. Funeral procession of Edward the Confessor approaching Westminster Abbey, from the Bayeux Tapestry

barely of the same status as the other great Benedictine houses at Bury St Edmunds or St Albans.'The years down to 1260 were lean' with no great accessions of property and some unwise policies on land management.[7] Although the Abbey possessed a patron saint buried within its walls after the canonization of the Confessor in 1161, it did not develop as a major centre of popular pilgrimage in any way rivalling the Shrine of St Thomas à Becket at Canterbury or the later shrines at Hailes and Walsingham.

The church of the Confessor is likely to have been modified during this period, perhaps by extension at the East End. The monks of Westminster probably shared the building fever which seized other institutions at the time. If the choir at Canterbury Cathedral could be extended and redeveloped twice in fifty years, it is likely that the choir at Westminster was treated in a similar fashion. There were important projects within the monastic complex, as for instance the erection of the Infirmary Chapel of St Katherine in the third quarter of the twelfth century. Henry II (1154–89) was reputed to have been a benefactor of the Abbey. But whatever was achieved in enhancing the Romanesque church, it is apparent that there was no significant increase during the twelfth century in either the size of the building or the area it covered.

Henry III's Rebuilding

In the 1240s, the fortunes of Westminster were again decisively changed by a monarch, this time by the Plantagenet King Henry III (1216–72). The building he created is generally discussed in terms of the introduction of the new style of Gothic to England and so it may seem strange to find it treated here as a work of 'restoration'. The standard literature dwells on its importance as an innovative building, and on the strength of the impact of French High Gothic on the Early English style. This is true in terms of the architectural style but not in terms of the Abbey's function. Henry III's patronage enhanced the status of the Abbey but did not change its essential role as a Benedictine monastery and a coronation church. While his own burial in Westminster set a pattern for later kings and further established the building as the royal mausoleum, it is not certain that this was Henry's original intention.

It is important to view the new works of Henry III, not as they are today, but as they would have been seen in his lifetime, embedded into a tight web of existing fabric belonging to both the Abbey and the Palace. His building occupied the same ground as its predecessor, sitting directly on top of it, to the extent of forcing an ingenious compromise on the south side whereby the west aisle of the South Transept straddles the east walk of the cloister. Perhaps it was simply too complicated to disturb the boundaries and buildings of both Palace and Abbey by attempting to obtain a more extensive area for the new scheme. The carved stones of the

3. Henry III, detail of tomb effigy

Romanesque church could be broken up and re-used as building materials (Cat. nos. 1 and 2), but it was evidently less easy for the designers of the new church to break out of the existing limitations on the site. It may even have been considered desirable for these links with the Confessor and the Conqueror to be respected.

To the south lay the monastic buildings which, except for the Chapter House, were left untouched until many years later. To the east rose the Lady Chapel, a substantial apsed building of at least six bays, founded by Abbot William de Humez in 1220 in response to the growing cult of the Virgin. Its construction did not necessarily imply any intention to rebuild the whole church. The Lady Chapel was preserved under Henry III's plan, although expensive alterations were made in 1256 to adapt it to the new scale of the church by raising the walls and re-roofing.[8] Behind the Lady Chapel rose the buildings of Westminster Palace, also improved and enlarged by the king.[9] Both in the Palace and in the Abbey, Henry III expressed his artistic ambitions through piecemeal additions of great internal splendour rather than by the imposition of a coherent new plan. The unusual attention given to the North Front of the North Transept may also reflect earlier patterns of use, rather than a new departure. The French-style triple portal was something of a sham: the easternmost portal was left blind (as it still remains) and the centre portal is likely to have formed a ceremonial entrance or *Porta Regia* reserved for special occasions, so that only the westernmost doorway was a standard route of access. These arrangements, so different from those of other great churches of the period, may be explained as a continuation of the patterns established during the Romanesque period.[10]

To the west of Henry's new church there remained substantial fragments of the Romanesque building. Even after the extension of the Gothic rebuilding in the later years of his reign to five bays west of the crossing, a further six bays as well as the West Towers remained standing. Although the Romanesque nave was almost certainly lower in height than the Gothic work, it would have formed an imposing mass, resembling more the mighty nave of the church of Jumièges than, for instance, the relatively humble fragment of the nave of about the year 1000 at Beauvais Cathedral. The Westminster nave survived for another hundred years, evidently being regarded as worth a considerable programme of repair well into the four-teenth century: between 1338 and 1343, over £150 were spent 'conducting the new work on the old church' (*facientes novum opus veteris ecclesiae*).[11]

Two points stand out in Henry III's rebuilding of Westminster which reinforced the distinct character of the building. First, the money financing the enterprise was provided almost entirely by the king. Colvin could only discover a single voluntary donation from another source and that was a legacy from the king's cousin, Archbishop Boniface.[12] Even the community at Westminster, which had their own resources, seem not to have made a voluntary contribution to the rebuilding programme. In 1258, however, the money they paid the king for the custody of their property during an interregnum between abbots was diverted to the building works. Thanks to the personal initiative of Abbot Richard de Ware, elected on that occasion, the Sanctuary and St Edward's Chapel were magnificently embellished with inlaid marble pavements placed by craftsmen brought from Rome working in the so-called Cosmatesque style. But this was a matter between the king and Abbot Ware and did not involve the monastery as a whole. The shields on the spandrels of the nave aisle arcading commemorate not donors but the wide extent of the king's matrimonial alliances.[13] The lack of financial support seems to have extended to Henry's own family. It is significant that although he honoured the Confessor by helping to bear the saint's body to its splendid new shrine in 1269, Edward I (1272–1307) felt unable to contribute significantly towards the completion of his father's design. Presumably he had a shrewd idea of the percentage of royal income which his father had devoted to the Abbey.

The second point is that considering Henry III's long involvement in the rebuilding programme—twenty-seven years—and the enormous sums he made available to his favourite project, the end results can be regarded as relatively meagre. The total expenditure was reckoned to have been more than £43,000, exclusive of the Shrine, while the contemporary presbytery at Ely cost just over £5,000.[14] In the years following the Conquest, vast new churches such as Christ Church, Canterbury or St Paul's, London had been completed in half the time. Earlier in the thirteenth century, Salisbury Cathedral was apparently built in thirty eight years. Yet by 1272, Henry III had achieved a half-finished church, which did not even have a central tower.

What Henry sought cannot have been size, for he was too discriminating a patron of the arts to be impressed merely by bulk. Royal money was spent on colour and richness: on the great variety of figurative carving and on the diaper ornament which covered, with unparalleled extravagance, the wall surfaces over the arcades and gallery of the apse, choir and transepts. Statues adorned the triple portal of the North Front, that gained the name of Solomon's Porch because of its splendour; censing angels were placed high up in the spandrels of the South Transept (Cat. no. 6; col.pl.VI); and equally fine though less conspicuous corbel heads were added at the gallery level (ills.5, 6). The Chapter House, completed between 1245 and 1253, was not only bold in its architecture but elaborately decorated with sculpture and a tiled floor similar to that Henry commissioned for his own palace at Clarendon, outside Salisbury.

An indication of the manner in which Henry III exercised his patronage can be seen in the construction of a new shrine for the Confessor, which was prepared over a period of almost thirty years. Such an object must always have been intended as the climax of the new building. But instead of rushing to complete the enterprise, Henry went to the trouble and expense, in 1252, of ordering the erection of a temporary chapel which was to be of suitable size and painted decoration to house the Shrine until the Sanctuary was ready to receive the relics of the saint. Also

MAUSOLEUM Sive FERETRUM Sti EDVARDI CONFESSORIS REGIS ANGLIÆ.

4. The Shrine of St Edward. Engraving by G. Vertue after J. Talman

significant is the fact that he spent large sums on building a massive bell tower to the north of the Abbey and on casting great bells for it as part of his initial programme of work at Westminster. Perhaps what Henry had in mind was to offer visitors the possibility to pass through Palace Yard to hear the bells, see both the Palace and the sculpted North Transept, and then enter the Abbey and worship at the Shrine. The visitor could leave without any need to venture westward down the nave, which could thus be left without embarrassment in its Romanesque form.

The vision Henry had for his church at Westminster was of a transcendent scale. Whatever his political limitations, he had wide artistic sympathies. The debate among later commentators about the extent of French or English influences on the Gothic employed by his masons would probably not have seemed relevant to him. Even when old and embattled, he could still be struck by the quality of the Italianate and ultimately classical style of the Cosmatesque school when he was introduced to it, presumably for the first time, by Abbot Ware's craftsmen. It is fitting that his own tomb, though constructed twenty years after his death, is in this rich and refined style, with its imperial and Roman resonances.

Henry seems to have conceived the Abbey as a double shrine, in which the glittering metal work of the Confessor's reliquary was enclosed within an outer shell of walls, carved and painted in a similar way. He was also keenly aware of the Abbey's role as the coronation church, where choir and crossing could be transformed into a stage on which the monarch is lifted high up for anointing and acclamation. This combination of ideas has indeed remained potent. As late as 1953, they could still come together at the Coronation of the present Queen, to striking effect.

5-6. Corbels from the gallery

7. Portrait of Richard II

The Medieval Abbey after Henry III

Royal enthusiasm for adorning or enlarging the Abbey waned dramatically after the death of Henry III, never to be resumed again to the same extent. Edward I (1272–1307) contributed little beyond the glazing of a few windows, and his son, Edward II (1307–27), only added a golden statue to the Shrine. Richard II (1377–99), with his devotion to St Edward, had been more generous, awarding £1,605 before his deposition. Henry V (1413–22) gave over twice as much, but his patronage ended with his early death. Henry VI (r. 1422–61 and 1470–71) diverted his efforts into his own new foundations at King's College, Cambridge, and at Eton, rather than completing the Abbey, even though it held the tombs of his parents and although he intended to be buried there as well.

The reconstruction of the Abbey resumed thanks to the generosity of a rich church-man rather than a sovereign. As in the case of the contemporary Abbey of the Vale Royal in Cheshire—magnificently begun but then abandoned by Edward I—it was a struggle for a religious community to continue works of royal scale from their own resources, without the benefit of significant royal patronage. It seems to have been the wealth and enthusiasm of Cardinal Langham, who had been Abbot from 1349 to 1362, rather than any initiative by Abbot Litlyngton and his monks, that prompted the rebuilding of the nave in 1376. The priority for these men lay in the rebuilding of the cloister and the monastic offices, as well as in the creation of a splendid abbot's house to the south-west of the church.[15] Accounts from the early fourteenth century reveal that substantial repairs were undertaken on the Romanesque parts of the nave. Strengthened in this way, the structure could have remained a stylistic hybrid until the present day, valued as much for the contrast between its parts as we prize its unity.

In 1387, the funds of the 'New Work', originally set aside for repairs to the monastic buildings following a disastrous fire in 1298, were diverted to the rebuilding of the nave. The young Richard II promised £100 a year and prompted—or at least permitted—the appointment of the leading royal mason, Henry Yevele, to superintend the works. By the time of his death, Yevele had completed the perimeter walls, the arcade piers and the lowest parts of the West Front. But, once again, Westminster suffered from the withdrawal of royal favour after the deposition of King Richard, and a lack of strong leadership within the monastery. Progress was slow over the following decades, although there was a sharp burst of activity under Henry V. Real activity began again after 1467, once Thomas Milling became Warden of the 'New Work' and then Abbot. There is evidence of a distinct fall in the value of the income enjoyed by both the abbot and convent in the early fifteenth century; and this fact may well have made the community cautious in pursuing elaborate building projects.

8. Head of Abbot Islip. Abbey Museum

The resumption of the work that had taken place in 1376 was marked by unusual architectural piety. Unlike the contemporary rebuilding of the naves at Winchester Cathedral or at Canterbury, where the Romanesque structures were stripped and reclothed in the Perpendicular, at Westminster it was decided to continue the style of Henry III's Gothic church. Some modifications were made, but they were subtle and sensitive, designed to respect what had gone before—not to correct it. The wall passages in the aisles were suppressed and the moulded capitals to the shafts were, in most cases, changed from round to polygonal. But the general lines of the elevation and the materials employed by Henry III's masons, including Purbeck marble, were maintained.

While not unique, this 'keeping in keeping' was exceptional for the period, especially for a major building in the heart of the capital, the nearest parallel being Beverley Minster in Yorkshire. Just a few yards to the east of the abbey church, St Stephen's Chapel in Westminster Palace, built by Edward I and Edward III as a disquieting rival to the Abbey, had offered masons the style of Perpendicular. At Westminster Abbey on the other hand, the masons chose not to follow the new style. Perhaps that same sense of regarding Westminster as a special case, which had limited its stylistic influence in the thirteenth century, sanctioned such conservatism over a hundred years later. There is no evidence that the decision taken at Westminster Abbey stimulated similar efforts at an 'Early English revival' in any other building. Christopher Wilson has argued that the main determining factor was the fact that, at Westminster, almost half of the thirteenth-century nave had already been built. Any change of style would have jarred, paralleling Wren's argument for stylistic conformity at Christ Church, Oxford, three hundred years later.[16]

By 1490, over a century after the resumption of construction on the nave, the 'New Work' had reached the stage of erecting the high vaults. The west window and towers remained, however, incomplete. There may have been a financial incentive

III. Polychrome Figure of Our Lady, *c.* 1300–1325 **[9]**

behind the Abbey's pursuit of its claim to house the body of Henry VI. This claim was probably prompted not only by a desire to honour the wishes of that unfortunate king, but also because of the development of St George's Chapel, Windsor, as an alternative royal burial place, which must have represented a severe threat to Westminster. Royal interest in the Abbey might dwindle and, with it, the chance of a speedy completion of the rebuilding programme. Moreover, the monks might also lose the endowments provided by the royal family for anniversary masses, which, by this period, gave a sizeable income to each member of the community. The Abbey's motive was desire for official support, rather than the installation of a new saint—for so Henry VI could be regarded—to promote pilgrimage. This is suggested by Westminster's apparent lack of interest in pursuing the translation of Henry VI's body, let alone his canonization, once the construction of the Henry VII Chapel was complete.

Although the Abbey proved successful in obtaining Henry VII's commitment to bury both Henry VI and himself in a sumptuous new chapel, it did not achieve royal support for the completion of the West Front of the church. By the time of Abbot Islip's death in 1532, the west window was complete and the nave and aisles vaulted, roofed and glazed. But the west gable was closed merely with weather-boarding and the flanking towers rose unevenly to just above roof level.

The new Lady Chapel built by Henry VII (1485–1509) to replace that founded almost three centuries before, was quite different from the rest of the abbey church.

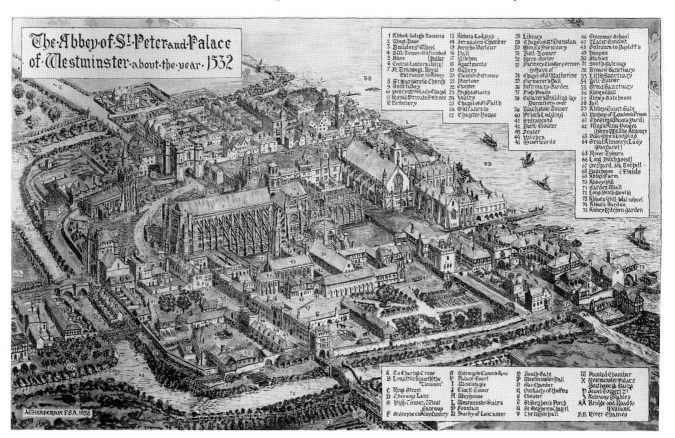

9. Westminster Abbey in the late Middle Ages. Reconstruction drawing by A. E. Henderson

IV *(left)*. Fragments of Stained Glass, *c.* 1250–1300 **[8]**

10. Fan vaulting in
the Henry VII Chapel

Structurally and stylistically, the new chapel stands distinct. The masons were not
interested in re-cladding or re-using the thirteenth-century shell, whether for reasons of sentiment or economy. Such fragmentary evidence of the earlier building as
survives has only been recovered by diligent scholarship.[17] The masons also had no
thought of adapting the style of their new design to that of Henry III's building,
whether in strict conformity with it, as in the nave, or in a more general agreement
in scale. The closest parallels are in the work carried out around the same period at
Windsor for the same patron. The undulating 'crinkle-crankle' of the aisle walls and
the ogee cupolas were surely designed both to recall Windsor and simultaneously
to eclipse it in splendour and bravura. This is even more true of the famous pendant
fan vault, technically more akin to examples at Christchurch Priory in Hampshire
and in the Divinity School at Oxford, but in terms of visual effect meant to outshine
the Yorkist kings' efforts at St George's Chapel, Windsor.

The construction of the chapel, though a royal work, was organized using a different administrative structure from that of Henry III's day. The money came from the king—as before—but the executive agent on the spot was the abbot, acting as royal official as well as head of his monastery. The grants from Henry VII were strictly controlled, as opposed to relying on whatever funds could be gathered in as chance directed. The indentures for the different stages of the building programme were well marshalled according to the standards of that business-like monarch. A final point of difference with the Plantagenet rebuilding was that, while Henry III was involved with the abbey church as a whole, his successor was primarily interested in his own contribution. The iconography of the elaborate decoration celebrated the concerns of the reigning dynasty rather than the achievements or traditions of the monastery's illustrious past. As prescribed in the king's will, 'all the holie companie of Heaven' found representation in the ranks of saints depicted throughout the church, both inside and out. Even more revealing of the king's underlying motivation was the injunction, superbly observed, that the decoration should be 'in as goodly and as riche maner as such a werk requireth, and as to a king's werk apperteignth.'[18]

11. Statues from the Henry VII Chapel (awaiting re-instatement in 1946)

12. Abbot Islip's Hearse before the High Altar. Islip Roll, 1532

II · From Reformation to Refoundation

Reformation and Dissolution

THE DEATH AND BURIAL of Abbot Islip in 1532, depicted in the famous illustrations to the funerary commemoration, known as the Islip Roll, are traditionally regarded as marking the end of medieval Westminster, and rightly so. Although Henry VIII (1509–47) did not approve of Protestant innovations in belief or liturgy, and although he had an elevated view of royal power, his reign witnessed the destruction of both the monastic community founded by the Confessor and the Confessor's Shrine. In 1536, the reliquary, with its metalwork and jewellery, was broken up and surrendered. The masonry sub-structure was probably dismantled as well; which would explain the present jumbled arrangement of its parts.[1] It would seem surprising for Henry to sanction the destruction of his famous predecessor's tomb; but he had little respect for the burial places of his medieval forbears, doing nothing to protect the tomb of Henry I (1100–35) at Reading Abbey or Stephen's (1135–54) at Faversham. Perhaps the intention was to remove the Shrine from its central position and then re-erect the base as a tomb somewhere less conspicuous. The demolition was done with sufficient care that the Confessor's body and the architectural components of the Shrine could be recovered without difficulty twenty years later.

In the years between 1540 and 1560, the status of the Abbey changed more frequently than ever before or since. From being a Benedictine monastery, it became the cathedral of a short-lived diocese of Westminster; after 1550, it served as a co-cathedral in the diocese of London; and in 1556 it changed to a Benedictine monastery again until it was refounded on 12 May 1560 as the Collegiate Church of St Peter. These drastic changes can have done little good to either the morale of the community or the well-being of the fabric. It is no coincidence that it was in 1546 that thieves took all the silver plates from the effigy of Henry V (1413–22), leaving only the wooden core.

Although the restored Benedictine community only occupied Westminster for less than three years, their Abbot, John Feckenham, was an energetic man who did much to bring back good order. His most prominent achievement was the restitution of the Confessor's Shrine. The speed of his work—a matter of months rather than years—meant that the result was not one of archaeological accuracy. Indeed,

13. The Shrine of St Edward, *c.* 1535. Reconstruction drawing by J.G. O'Neilly

14. Coronation of Henry VIII, showing building in progress on the West Towers. Islip Roll, 1532

later scholars should be grateful that he did not deem it right to spend more time and money on a new shrine, since a more elaborate restoration would presumably have been in a classical style, dispensing with Henry III's thirteenth-century work. The wooden canopy over the masonry base is designed as two superimposed orders of pilasters and arcading, owing something to contemporary Renaissance furnishings typical of Northern Italy.[2]

The efforts of Queen Mary I (1553–58) and Abbot Feckenham to restore old ways did not long survive the accession of Elizabeth I (1558–1603). The second dissolution and the transfer of the Abbey from Feckenham to his successors were conducted in a civilized manner; but, even so, the future must have seemed bleak. In the event, Elizabeth copied her sister's initiative by refounding the Abbey as a unique institution, although she laid greater stress on education rather than on liturgical observance, as for example the links she established between Westminster School, Christ Church, Oxford, and Trinity College, Cambridge. Indeed, Elizabeth can worthily take her place alongside the Confessor and Henry III as a major benefactor of the Abbey (see Cat. no. 17).

15. The Islip Chapel. Islip Roll, 1532

V *(left)*. Angel with Harp,
c. 1255–1260 [**5**]

VI *(below)*. Cast of thirteenth-century Censing Angel
from Spandrel in South Transept [**6**]

VII to VIII *(overleaf)*. Statues of
St Katherine and St Matthew
from the Henry VII Chapel, *c.* 1510 [**13**]

left). Fragments of Stained Glass, *c.* 1250–1300 [**8**]

IX & X. Effigy of Queen Elizabeth I,
and the original undergarment, 1603 and 1760 [**17**]

Refoundation

While the forty-year reign of Dean Goodman, from 1561 to 1601, consolidated the Elizabethan settlement at Westminster, it is hard to identify any intervention on the fabric during this period of time. Two of his successors in the early seventeenth century, Richard Neile and then John Williams, are documented as generous and energetic patrons. Williams instigated a restoration in the 1620s which began at the south-east corner of the Abbey. This part of the Abbey seemed to be 'the more deformed with decay because it coupled with a later building . . the Henry VII Chapel, which was tight and fresh.' Yet the more exposed parts to the north-west were also in a bad state. 'The great buttresses which were almost crumbled to dust with the injuries of the weather, he re-edified with durable materials and beautified with elegant statues (among whom Abbot Islip had a place) so that £4,500 was spent in a trice.'[3] Although doctrinally more conservative than his hated rival Archbishop Laud, Williams combined his work on the Abbey's fabric with a revived 'beauty of holiness' in the church services. A visiting French priest could congratulate him on the order and richness of their conduct.[4]

Although Williams clung stubbornly to the Deanery—resisting relentless attacks by Charles I (1625–49) and Laud—and although he enjoyed a temporary triumph in 1641 with his translation to the archbishopric of York, his achievements were swept away by the onset of the Civil War. The Chapter continued meeting until May 1642, but its worship and even its corporate identity were abolished soon thereafter, not to be reinstated until 1660. Westminster would have appeared an obvious victim of the Civil Wars, marked for destruction as a monument too closely associated with monks and monarchs. There was, indeed, the notorious episode in 1644 when the Parliamentarian Speaker of the House of Commons, Sir Robert Harley, 'cleansed' the Abbey and is reputed to have personally smashed the touchstone altar slab of the monument to Edward VI (1547–53) in the Henry VII Chapel.[5] A year earlier, in the summer of 1643, soldiers perpetrated the same kind of pantomime mockery of the Anglican service carried out in other cathedrals such as Lichfield, Norwich and Chichester, when the organ, the liturgical books and the vestments were desecrated and destroyed.

However, the striking feature is the care with which the Abbey was preserved by the Parliamentary regime. Between 1643 and 1649 it allowed the Assembly of Presbyterian divines to meet in the Abbey buildings, which was responsible, among other things, for the famous Westminster Confession. Far from causing harm to the Abbey, this episode in its history has given glory to the name Westminster in circles far removed from the Anglican Communion. Although there were isolated instances of iconoclasm, there was no wholesale destruction of either images or monuments. Nor were there any proposals, as for instance at Lichfield Cathedral, to take the church down as superfluous and sell its materials. The valuable bronze of the effigies and grille of Henry VII's tomb did not follow the ancient Crown Jewels into the melting pot to provide funds for the hard-pressed Commonwealth Treasury.

Dr Armitage Robinson, Dean of Westminster at the beginning of this century and no Low Churchman, admitted' that never were the finances of the Abbey more carefully handled...Every item of expenditure was noted, every voucher kept.'[6] A Board of Governors took the place of the Dean and Chapter, and they were proud enough of their position to commission a handsome seal, designed by Thomas Symons (or Simon), showing the House of Commons on one side and the North Transept and its Great Porch on the other side.

Restoration of King and Chapter

Despite the care of the Governors, the fabric was evidently in need of attention by the time the King and the Dean and Chapter returned to power in 1660. In September of that year Samuel Pepys was 'afeared' when 'in the midst of sermon some plaster fell from the top of the Abbey.'[7] There was an energetic response from the reinstated Dean and Chapter, since between 1660 and 1661, £2,314 was spent on the fabric, out of a total of £3,930 allocated to refitting the church.[8] However, details are sparse regarding what seems to have been the major task: the alterations to the North Front

16. The North Front, c. 1654. Engraving by Hollar

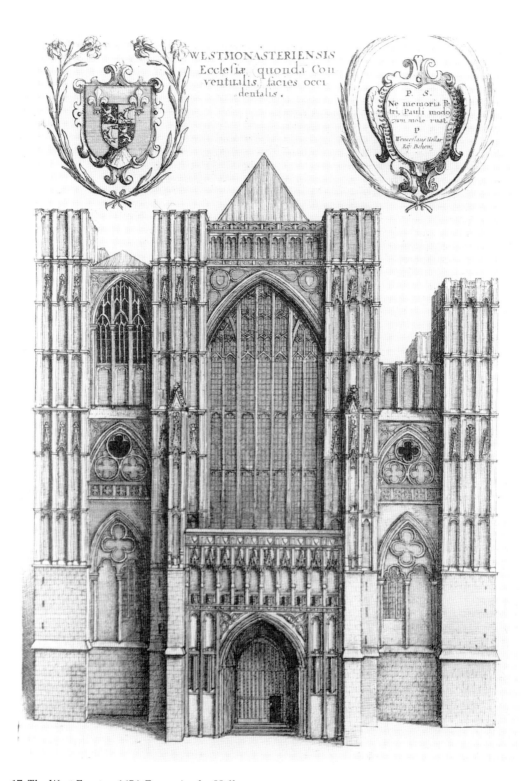

WESTMONASTERIENSIS
Ecclesiæ quonda Con
ventualis, facies occi
dentalis.

P. S.
Ne memoria Pe
tri, Pauli modo
cum mole ruat.
P
Wenceslaus Hollar
Eq Bohem.

17. The West Front, c. 1654. Engraving by Hollar

after the removal of the outer porch, which had been added around 1360 and which was probably demolished in the 1660s.[9] In addition, what Wren later called 'a little Doric passage' with a kind of portico of round-headed arches under a battlemented parapet, was set under the great rose window in place of the continuous Gothic arcading. A recent commentator has called this 'the merest butchery', but this is to adopt an anachronistic standpoint.[10] To update the fabric following a contemporary style could be seen as a tribute to the Abbey rather than any sign of disrespect. Another group of alterations which can be attributed to this time is the work carried out on the South Transept, where the rose window was repaired and the turrets were given ogee caps or cupolas.[11] While similar ogee caps formerly on the West Front of Norwich Cathedral can be dated to about 1700, it is unlikely that such a motif would have been adopted at Westminster after Wren's appointment in 1699.

It is hard to establish how much responsibility for decisions on design or even demolition rested with the surveyors of the Abbey during the years after 1660. Edward (or Robert) Woodroffe, who held office from 1662 to 1675,[12] is not credited with any major commission, but he must have been an architect of some reputation since he was appointed one of the three surveyors to rebuild the City churches after the Great Fire, together with two of his eventual successors at the Abbey, Robert Hooke and Christopher Wren. There is no evidence to connect any one of them with the demolition of the outer north porch. Hooke, who was Surveyor to the Dean and Chapter in the 1690s, was consulted about the repair of the choir in 1676 and, seventeen years later, about work on the exterior.[13] It is tempting to attribute to Hooke—architect of such important works as Montagu House in London—rather than to Woodroffe, the late seventeenth-century refashioning of the pulpitum or choir screen. Its unusual mixture of elements makes it unlikely to be the work of Wren. Moreover, the latter only began to repair the Abbey in the last year of the century. The walls of the pulpitum facing down the nave were left unadorned, but the central entry was flanked by large pylons of a very original design, with tall classic piers topped by tapering pyramids (Cat. no. 22), evocative of the Gothic style.

Despite these various interventions, a survey of January 1696–97 found 'the wants of repairing to be so great and all its [the Abbey's] parts so very defective that unless speedy care be taken they will require a much greater charge.' Roofs, windows, buttresses and vaults were all in need of urgent attention. The estimate was over £30,000.[14]

The resources of the Dean and Chapter were unable to provide anything approaching this sum. Fortunately, a precedent had been established when a proportion of the Coal Tax had been assigned to rebuild the City of London churches and St Paul's Cathedral. With the aid of Charles Montagu, Chancellor of the Exchequer and an old Westminster boy himself, an Act of Parliament was passed in 1697 to permit such a grant towards the 'repairing and finishing' of the abbey church. This provided the mainspring of the work, although it had to be followed by a further

18. The South Transept in 1807. Anonymous drawing

five Acts since the original estimates proved unrealistic.[15] For this distinguished work, equally distinguished officers were required. They included four Chief Justices and the Chancellor of the Exchequer amongst the Commissioners, and a new Chief Surveyor, with twice the salary of the traditional Surveyor to the Dean and Chapter, in the person of Sir Christopher Wren.

19. Dickinson's design for the restoration of the North Transept, 1719, approved by Wren

III · The Great Restoration of Wren and Hawksmoor, 1699–1745

T HE RESTORATION of Westminster Abbey inaugurated by the Parliamentary grant of 1697 lasted for almost fifty years and constituted the most prominent and costly restoration project of its day. Indeed, its sensitivity towards the existing medieval fabric was exceptional for its time, not only in Britain but in any part of Europe. It also has a particular interest, since the principal architects involved— Christopher Wren, William Dickinson and Nicholas Hawksmoor—have all left evidence of their understanding of medieval architecture. Wren and Hawksmoor wrote papers explaining in detail the restoration projects they were undertaking and the principles by which they were guided.[1]

Towards the end of Queen Anne's reign, the aims behind this undertaking were proclaimed to be 'the honour of God, the spiritual welfare of Her Majesty's subjects, the interests of the established Church and the glory of Her Majesty's reign.'[2] Such sentiments, especially when expressed in the tangible form of financial support for the building work from the Government, reflected assumptions concerning the mutual roles of Church and State characteristic of their period. Such Tory assumptions could appear doubtful by the time the programme ended in the Whig age of William Kent and the young Horace Walpole, and they would have seemed obsolete by the time the Victorian restorations began a century later.

Wren and Dickinson

The first instalment of the Parliamentary grant was paid on 30 December 1700. During the following decade, efforts were concentrated on the windows, roofs and buttresses on the south side, which was not encumbered by the houses which had been built along the north side. The emphasis at this stage was on simple repair. The windows appear to have been replaced with little alteration except for a simplification of the mouldings: the jambs of the windows on the east side of the North Transept were flattened into chamfers and those on the outer windows on the south side were replaced by a single broad hollow.[3] The cost per window—including glass, iron and stonework—was reckoned at £50.[4] Some of the ancient stained glass from around the church was repaired and gathered in the apse windows in 1703. But it is clear from drawings that some lights in upper windows were blocked with plaster and brickwork (Cat. no. 32).

The other major task of this decade was the repair of the roofs. This comprised the piecemeal patching and replacement of individual timbers and the introduction of new trusses to support the thirteenth-century frames and their securing by means of iron bolts, keys and collars. The major problem was that the thirteenth-century roofs consisted of trussed rafters with tie-beams at intervals but no principal trusses or purlins. For this reason, strutting had to be introduced in the presbytery and in the South Transept in order to prevent their roofs from tilting outwards. In addition, tie-beams were strengthened with bolts to keep them from 'sagging' down onto the vaulting. Only the fifteenth-century roof at the west end of the nave was sufficiently secured by its original crown-brace and collar purlins not to require additional struts.[5]

A major diversion of time and effort during the first decade of the restoration was caused by Queen Anne's gift, in 1706, of the elaborate altarpiece from her father's Roman Catholic Chapel in Whitehall, redundant since James II's flight in 1688 and homeless since the fire of 1698 (see Cat. no. 20). It was a work of exceptional quality, designed by Wren and adorned with statues and reliefs by Arnold Quellin and Grinling Gibbons. It must have given Wren and Gibbons great satisfaction to find a suitable home for what had been one of their major achievements, although the original design was evidently adjusted in shape and iconography to fit its new position.

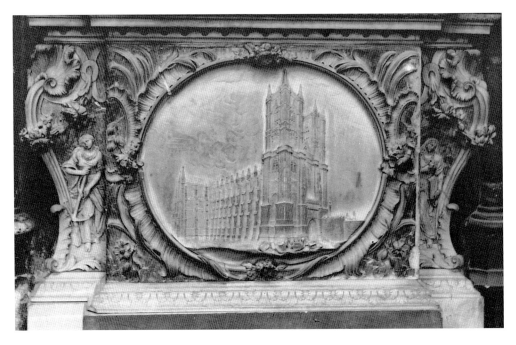

20. Relief showing the new West Towers, from the monument to Dean Wilcocks (died 1756)

XI. Portraits of Philip and Mary from the Charter of 1556 [16]

XII. Design for Spires on the West Towers by Nicholas Hawksmoor

21. Detail of medieval roofs, before reconstruction

The Dean and Chapter hoped to pay for the installation of the altarpiece from the Parliamentary grant under the heading of 'repairs'. As Samuel Barton wrote to the Treasurer in 1710, '…'tis true 'tis not such repairs as were necessary to prevent the fabric from becoming wholly ruinous which is expressed to be the intention of the Parliament in giving us the money. But however I do not think they intended to confine us merely to that, but that they intended…the Church should be made very decent and handsome.'[6] The Treasurer maintained that this was a 'misapplication' of the grant, which was only meant for the 'support of the main building.' There was nothing to spare for fittings.[7]

The installation of the altarpiece cost a good £500 and came near to causing the destruction of the precious thirteenth-century Cosmatesque paving in the Sanctuary. However, the structure was not the aesthetic disaster which some later writers have claimed. Not only were the carving and the materials of the finest quality—as is demonstrated by surviving fragments at Burnham-on-Sea (Cat. no. 20)—but the towering structure must have restored to the building something of the focus provided in pre-Reformation times by the tall rood and the elevated reliquary chest

ANNA REGINA PIA FELIX

The Altar of Westminster Abbey

22. Wren's 'Whitehall' Altarpiece. Engraving, 1808

of the Confessor's Shrine. The insertion of furnishings in a contemporary classical style argued no disrespect for the medieval architecture of the fabric.

In the second decade of the restoration project, attention moved to repairing the most decayed part of the building: the north side, especially the North Transept and its porch. In 1683, H. Keepe had described the appearance of the North Front as 'rather the skeleton of the church than any great comeliness' due to the ill-effects of coal smoke and the north winds, although at that stage some statues still remained surrounding the thirteenth-century portals.[8] Wren described its condition in some detail in his famous 'memorial' of 1713 to Dean Atterbury. The great rose window was partly blocked with plaster and the 'little Doric passage' had been added beneath it. The 'pyramids' (pinnacles) had been cropped off and the staircases covered with 'very improper roofs of timber and lead which can never agree with any other part of the design.' Wren aimed 'to restore it to its proper shape first intended.'[9]

Ten years later, the Abbey's Under-Surveyor, William Dickinson, succeeded in carrying out Wren's intentions, clearing away incongruities and restoring the Gothic detail. It is an extraordinarily significant moment in the history of restoration. Not only was Gothic retained for reasons of stylistic conformity, but there was a deliberate intention to research and reinstate the original design. From here it was a short step to the attempts of James Essex, in his restorations at Lincoln Cathedral in the 1770s, to make his designs 'as near as I could agreeable to the ideas' of the first architect.[10]

Three elements of the work as executed have remained controversial. The most serious was the paring away of the remains of the 'time-eaten' thirteenth-century sculpture on the portals of the North Front. According to Baker King, a mason who worked for George Gilbert Scott in the restoration of the 1870s, 'the orders of the arches were reworked to cut away the carving, with large hollow Purbeck abaci cut away so as to have less overhang,' following a treatment similar to that carried out on the window mouldings.[11] Scott himself called Wren's capitals 'huge ungainly acorns.'[12] But to the early eighteenth-century eye, it made sense to remove decayed and unsightly stone work—however splendid it might once have been—so as to restore something of the 'magnificence' proper to the porch.

Other alterations to what has been reconstructed as the original thirteenth-century design were less serious. The separate gabled roofs of the three portals were replaced by one single parapet roof, more consonant with contemporary taste, but also making good any scars left by the removal of the fourteenth-century outer porch.[13] Much more prominent, and certainly approved by Wren, was the placing of a tall pinnacle on the gable apex instead of the cross shown in Hollar's engraving of about 1650, which combined with the angle pinnacles to give a curious three-pronged outline to the transept.[14] This might be explained in part by contemporary reluctance to display a cross for fear of superstition and popery, and in part by

23. Example of 'acorn' moulding
from the Wren restoration on the north apsidal chapel

Wren's desire to give greater interest to the Abbey's skyline. The arcading under the rose window mentioned above, was replaced by a sympathetically Gothic equivalent but, as Lethaby pointed out, the rhythm of the openings was now made 3:5:3, instead of the original 2:4:2.

Perhaps the most striking aspect of the restoration for contemporaries was the reinstatement of tracery in the rose window with its lights being cleared of plaster and now filled with new stained glass.[15] This depicted the Apostles and the Four Evangelists after cartoons by Sir James Thornhill (Cat. no. 28; col. pl. XV). When Dean Atterbury—whose enthusiasm had promoted the restoration—was forced into exile through plotting with the Jacobites, his one request was to see the rose window complete with its glass before he left England. Another sign of the importance attached to this part of the restoration was that Dickinson, who died in 1725, was buried just outside the North Front, under an inscription proudly commemorating his leading role in the restoration.[16]

Hawksmoor

When Nicholas Hawksmoor succeeded as Surveyor of the Abbey in 1723 he did not simply continue the work of his predecessors. He tackled the architectural and administrative problems of the restoration with a fresh mind. Although work had been in progress for over twenty years, a vast amount remained to be done: on the western part of the church, a great deal on both sides of the nave and on the Henry VII Chapel.

Hawksmoor's surveyorship is as memorable for the 'finishing' as it is for the 'repairing' of the building. An estimate made by Dickinson in January 1724 for the 'remaining repairs' already included £8,500 for a crossing tower rising 90 feet above the roof and crowned by a dome and lantern; £7,000 for raising the West Towers; £5,000 for a new choir; and £8,560 for clearing away the houses built along the north side of the church.

In retrospect, the only time when the erection of a crossing tower was a serious possibility was in the mid 1720s. In his memorial of 1713, Wren thought that 'the original intention was plainly to have had a steeple;' not so much because of aesthetic considerations, but because he believed that the weight of the steeple would help anchor the crossing. In visual terms, he claimed that a spire would give 'a proper grace to the whole fabric, and the west end of the City, which seems to want it.'[17] Although he had a model constructed, we do not know for certain which design he found most suitable (Cat. no. 24). An engraving by Fourdrinier, which purported to show Wren's intentions, was not published until 1737—over a decade after the latter's death—and does not correspond with any of the alternative designs shown in the surviving drawings by either Dickinson or Hawksmoor. Wren's declared purpose was to 'agree with the original scheme of the old architect without any modern mixture to show my own inventions.' However, the schemes drawn by Dickinson in late 1722 or early 1723[18] derive less inspiration from medieval examples and rather more from Wren's designs for Old St Paul's and for his rebuilding of it after the Great Fire. One of Dickinson's drawings [19] shows an octagonal drum pierced by two tiers of trefoil openings supporting a sixteen-sided dome ribbed by crockets.

Hawksmoor continued to favour the 'dome and lantern' idea which had already appeared in Dickinson's drawing of September 1722[20] and which had been costed in his January 1724 estimate.[21] By the time the revised estimates were prepared in November of that year, the idea of a steeple must have been abandoned since they refer to the placing of 'a new basement and upon that a lantern in the middle of the church, where the mid steeple was at first intended.'[22] Hawksmoor envisaged something along the lines of the lantern and ogee cupola he had designed for Beverley Minster in about 1720 and which were later removed. In a letter written to

A Perspective View of the Collegiate Church of S.ᵗ Peter Westminster with the Towers & Spire as Design'd by S.ᵗ Christer

24. Engraving of 1737 showing Wren's proposal for a spire, after Fourdrinier

25. Engraving of the North Front, *c.* 1793

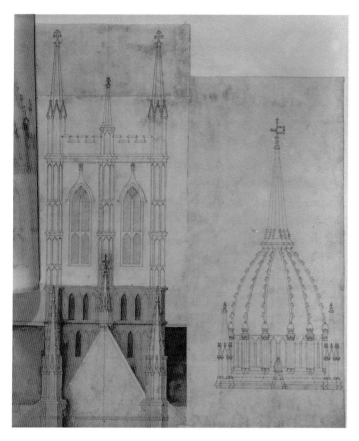

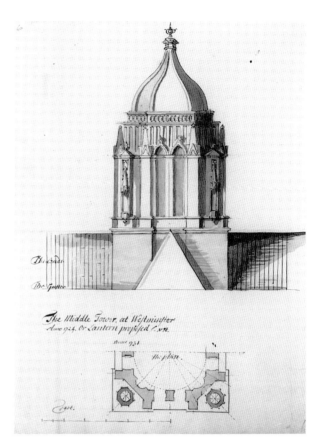

26. Dickinson's studies for a polygonal 'dome', and for a square tower over the crossing

27. Hawksmoor's design and plan for a proposed lantern

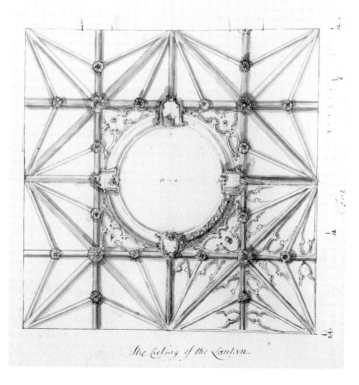

28. Hawksmoor's design for the ceiling of the proposed lantern

Dean Wilcocks in January 1736, he discussed how at Beverley they 'finished the middle lantern, which was left at ye height of ye gutter, but we rais'd it as high as our money would reach, and covered it in the form of a Gothic cupola.'[23] He therefore still hoped that some form of cupola might yet be erected, even though the internal work on the crossing had already been completed in 1727.[24]

The recent discovery of further designs by Hawksmoor for the central and western towers of the Abbey and for possible alterations to the choir shed more light on Hawksmoor's contribution (Cat. no. 25). The restoration of the crossing led to further work in the choir which lay beneath it.[25] The eastern arm over the Sanctuary had been extensively repaired in around 1700 and the decorative painting of the vault had been reinstated. Thirty years later, the woodwork in the choir was thoroughly repaired—in 1732, joiners were paid £11 for 63 feet of 'revealed "gothick" work in pilasters and backs of the arches'—and the choir screen reconstructed.[26] King George II's gift of an organ in 1728 made it necessary to replace the two piers flanking the central gateway of the screen with a more conventional arch which could support the instrument.[27] Hawksmoor prepared a classical design in the Doric order [28] similar to his gallery fronts at Beverley Minster; but it was his 'Gothic' design which was approved on 1 June 1728. Its main feature was 'an obtuse arch resting on triplicated pillars, terminated by pinnacles in Kent's style' and, within the vestibule, a vault of a 'large circle enclosing a quatrefoil with a rose in the centre and rays in the corners.'[29] The blind faces of the flanking walls were altered when the monuments of Isaac Newton and Lord Stanhope, carved by Rysbrack after Kent's designs, were added in 1731 and 1733 respectively. The monuments were set flat against the wall (not as now in niches), and were framed above by battlement-like steps in the parapet. The choice of these two modern heroes for such a prominent position was no accident. Their monuments can be seen as either a post-Reformation equivalent of the altars traditionally flanking the rood-screen door or as the commemoration of two modern exemplars of the Active and Contemplative Life.

These years had seen an especially acute crisis in the payment of the Parliamentary grant. Yet by March 1732 work could start on the crowning effort, the completion of the West Front, thanks to some easing in the financial situation and to the appointment of Joseph Wilcocks, Bishop of Gloucester, as Dean. He made the completion of the restoration his main task during the twenty-five years he governed the Abbey. An estimate of March 1732 allowed £11,000 for finishing the West Towers, complete with their windows and their returns to the nave, although further repairs costing nearly £10,000 still had to be completed on the nave.[30] The first part of the task, in 1733–34, was to repair the existing fabric of the West End. The great window was 'quite ruinous', and the gable above it was boarded. Moreover, 155 feet of the roof had to be repaired.[31] By midsummer 1734, masons' work costing over £800 had been carried out on the head of the west window, the

29. Hawksmoor's classical design for the Choir Screen

29. Sir Isaac Newton. ENTRANCE into the CHOIR. 30. Earl of Stanhope.

30. Hawksmoor's design for the Choir Screen, as executed. Engraving, 1812

cornice and the balustrade.[32] Hawksmoor considered a variety of designs for the West Front which included new tracery in the window and a new entry. He ultimately chose to retain the late medieval detailing, refacing the masonry where necessary in Portland stone. He was not afraid to add contemporary features such as the coats of arms and niche canopies over the portal and the prominent inscription recording King George II and the date of 1735 over the window.

The West Towers had been abandoned unfinished just above the eaves line of the nave roof at the time of Abbot Islip. The north west tower, containing the bells, was a stage higher than the other, giving a curious lop-sided impression to a composition which should have rivalled the North Front as the major public entry to the Abbey. After again experimenting with a variety of solutions, Hawksmoor decided to maintain the same general plan but narrowed the upper dimensions. The result resembles the twin-towered West Front of Beverley Minster the restoration of which he had supervised between 1716 and 1720. Those Gothic details not taken from the existing fabric at Westminster seem also to have derived from Beverley, in particular the traceried panelling of the buttresses and the ogee hood moulds of the belfry openings. By 1738, the north west tower was approaching completion, including all the carved detail, mostly by John Boson, who provided 'foliage', 'crockets', and the tympana with 'Time's Head and wings' and 'festoons etc. 8 feet long.'[33]

By now Hawksmoor was dead. John James, who, since the death of Dickinson had been Surveyor of the College (i.e. all the buildings owned by the Dean and Chapter, excluding the church), now took his place as Surveyor of the Fabric. James may have lacked the genius of Hawksmoor, but he was a competent and conscientious architect, well suited to complete the towers. He could tactfully explain to the Treasurer a dispute over pay because it was impossible to measure Gothic work from drawings and very difficult even 'when wrought', because of its 'windings and turnings.'[34] James finished the south west tower by 1744 and the long programme of work was deemed complete the following year, although no proper restoration of the Henry VII Chapel had been carried out. The last grant was voted in 1743 and a full account was laid before Parliament in March 1745.[35]

The final cost of 'repairing and finishing' the Abbey amounted to about £100,000 without including a central spire or cupola. In 1724 the cost of the restoration, together with 'new additions' including a central spire, had been estimated at £58,441, on top of the £49,000 already spent between 1699 and 1717.[36] The Abbey was supposed to receive £4,000 per annum from the Parliamentary grant; but this seemingly generous provision was never sufficient, mainly because the money was usually paid in such arrears that deficits accumulated and the new income was spent paying off debts from previous years. Already by 1708 it had to be ordered that no more than £1,000 should be spent on the fabric in the coming year and the rest 'applied towards the payment of the moneys borrowed on the credit of the Act.'[37] In the 1720s the Abbey authorities tried to take over funds that had been allocated

The West Front and the the Great window as, now in a Sad Ruinous and unfinished Condition. an⁰ 1731.

31. Hawksmoor's drawing of the unfinished West Front, *c.* 1731

32. Hawksmoor's design
for the West Window

by Parliament in 1711 to the building of the Fifty New Churches. They argued that, since only twelve were being built, the 'surplus' could be used on the Abbey, giving preference to 'preserving a noble fabric' rather than to 'the building of a new parish church or two.' By means of some ingenious arithmetic, they demonstrated that the public would only be losing one church.[38]

Parliament was increasingly unwilling to continue the grant, especially after the Whigs re-established their dominance with the Hanoverian Succession. As a result, there were periodic crises in 1717, 1724 (the Great Stand), 1731, 1737, and 1743 when the Dean and Chapter had to go cap-in-hand to the House of Commons to prevent the cancellation of the restoration programme. The principal complaint from the Commons was that the Abbey's own revenues from its estates and from the fees charged at burials and for monuments were enough to enable the prebends to contribute more generously to the restoration. To modern minds this seems reasonable since the holders of the Westminster stalls generally enjoyed other preferments as well: in 1722, at least two canons held bishoprics, apart from the Dean who, by tradition, combined Westminster with the ill-endowed see of Rochester. But, as the Dean and Chapter never ceased to point out, not only had the fabric been admitted since 1662 to a permanent 'dividend' or share in the fines from leases as they arose, but the fabric consisted of more than just the church and the Canons' houses. The former monastic buildings, a number of which were now appropriated for the use of Westminster School, were a heavy charge. In the forty years from 1660 to 1700, £8,218 had been spent on 'several public buildings and places within the College,' which included the Prebends' houses. In the next forty years, the total rose to nearly £20,000, of which most was spent on Westminster School.[39] The building of the great dormitory designed by Lord Burlington helped to swell this latter sum.[40]

The defence advanced by the Dean and Chapter for the payment of a £4,000 grant a year of public money for their restoration project was that they wanted no 'advantage for themselves but only the munificence of Parliament to finish and repair a public building consecrated for religious worship and which also is the place of the coronation…and of the sepultures of many of the nobility and gentry.'[41] They stressed that 'the said church (which was never finished) came into the hands of the first Dean and Chapter with the towers half-built, and without any appropriation of fabric rents either for finishing it or repairing it.' Above all, the fact that Parliament had voted money for the restoration in the past showed that 'it was considered a public affair, and not the concern only of a private Dean and Chapter.'[42] The architectural quality of the building was hardly mentioned except for general references to it being 'one of the most ancient and magnificent buildings in this kingdom.'[43] It was the focal point of the Abbey in national life that justified its special treatment.

Looking at the issue the other way, why did Parliament continue to pay the grants? The principal reason must have been that the Abbey was considered as much a public building as a church. With the emergence of Britain as a great power during the reigns of William III (1689–1702) and Anne (1702–14), it was necessary to enhance the appearance of the capital. As von Uffenbach noticed in 1710, the fact that the royal place of coronation and burial was not only in decay but unfinished was an obvious reproach.[44] The continuing shift of influential residents to London's West End and the transformation of Whitehall after the 1698 fire from a royal palace to a street of aristocratic houses meant that Westminster had become a more elegant part of London.[45] Nor must the proximity of the Abbey to the Houses of Parliament

33. Dated rainwater head

be forgotten, even though a crowd of buildings still clustered between them. Members could use their own eyes to test the truth of the Chapter's claims.

The accession of the Hanoverian dynasty enhanced the status of the Abbey. The Henry VII Chapel continued to serve as the royal mausoleum and also gained the role of Chapel of the Knights of the Bath once the Order was re-established in 1725. New stalls faithfully replicating the original ones had to be added in order to accommodate the new complement of Knights. Canaletto's painting of 1749, showing the Knights of the Bath in solemn procession out of the gleaming new West Front, aptly symbolises this aspect of the restoration (col. pl. XIII).

The Replacement of the Choir in 1775

It is typical of the way attitudes towards the past were changing in the eighteenth century that the Abbey authorities passed from a concern to restore and complete the fabric to a desire to re-fashion it for practical reasons. The plan, in the early 1770s, to move the choir would have altered the interior of the building more radically than either the Reformation or the Civil War had achieved.

34. The Choir and Presbytery. Engraving, *c.* 1785

There were two underlying reasons for altering the arrangement of the choir, one utilitarian and the other visual. The Coronation of George III in 1761 had been so mismanaged, that the young Earl Marshal tactlessly remarked to the equally young monarch that next time he would see things were better done. The event also yielded over £1,000 which was voted by the Chapter in 1763 to be 'laid out in the alterations intended to be made in the quire.'

It was proposed that the inflexible thirteenth-century canopied stalls enclosed by stone walls running parallel to the aisles should be replaced by stalls which could be dismantled when required, making the erection of the necessary staging at coronations much less complicated. The question then arose of whether to place the new stalls in the traditional site athwart the crossing or east of it, filling the east arm. This would have entailed removing both the fifteenth-century altar screen and the Confessor's Shrine. On the other hand, it would have had the advantage of concentrating the regular worship of the community in one space, without the choir and Sanctuary being separated by the crossing and transepts which dispersed all the sound and heat. At around this time, such a move was actually carried out at Ely Cathedral to general acclaim.[46]

The Dean, John Thomas, discussed the matter widely. Horace Walpole, so prominent in the Gothic Revival, recommended a dramatic scheme in which a high altar, enclosed by an octagonal canopy on the model of the market crosses at Chichester or Salisbury, would be placed as a kind of 'eye-catcher' in the apse. Professional advice was sought in May 1773 from three architects: Henry Keene, Surveyor of the Abbey since 1752; James Wyatt, the rising architectural star of the day and soon to succeed Keene; and James Essex, author of the successful scheme at Ely. Sadly, the competing designs have never been traced. But their flavour may be suggested in sketches drawn by Essex preserved in the British Library.[47] He planned a lofty Gothic altarpiece similar to the one he had installed at Lincoln Cathedral and a west gallery and organ at the crossing. The fate of the Confessor's Shrine and of the other monuments around the apse is not indicated.

After a prolonged debate, conservatism won the day and it was resolved to ask Keene to refurnish the choir but retaining its traditional site. The number of stalls was dramatically reduced, but the layout retained a wide centre aisle.[48] Plans exist of the former stalls, but no elevation drawings were ever made, so we know little of the detail of their construction. Two misericords have survived, one formerly in the Museum and now in store, and other re-used in the stalls of the Henry VII Chapel, ironically alongside eighteenth-century neo-medieval examples.

XIII. Procession of Knights of the Bath at Westminster Abbey. Painting by Canaletto, 1749

XIV. View of the Henry VII Chapel from Old Palace Yard (detail)
Water-colour by Thomas Malton Jr., 1796. Coll. Donald Buttress [35]

The Restoration of the Henry VII Chapel

By the end of the century it was clear that a considerable sum would have to be spent on the Henry VII Chapel. Although it had been included in the estimates for both Wren's and Hawksmoor's restorations, little or nothing had been achieved, presumably because the construction of the West Towers seemed a greater priority for the Parliamentary grant. In 1793 the roofs were repaired at a cost of £1,900 and the Surveyor, James Wyatt, did a trial restoration of the area over the window at the East End. However, the Chapter's preparations were interrupted in July 1803 by a near-disastrous fire in the roofs caused by plumbers' negligence which destroyed the lantern and threatened the entire building. The church was saved—in part—by the *trompe-l'oeil* paintings on canvas of traceried rose windows, attached as decoration to the Hawksmoor timber vaulting in the lantern during the Keene restoration, which held back the flames.[49] Amongst the repairs was a panelled ceiling to the lantern by Wyatt, much reviled in later times because it was of plaster and therefore considered as bogus or temporary, but evidently a sound example of its date and type. The costs amounted to £3,848, absorbing the funds originally intended for the repair of the Henry VII Chapel.

Thus, for a second time, the Abbey had recourse to Parliament for additional grants. The then Dean's version of how this money was obtained stressed the personal intervention of Lord Grenville. However, such a development would have been a natural part of the major programme of public improvements being sponsored at the time in the Westminster area, particularly around the Palace and the bridge. It has been estimated that £250,000 of public money was spent around Old Palace Yard, St Margaret's Church and the Sanctuary during this period.[50] Moreover, it can hardly be a coincidence that negotiations for the grant for the Henry VII Chapel were under way just at the time that Wyatt executed his new frontage of the House of Lords, exactly opposite the Abbey. Also relevant is the fact that the Houses of Parliament granted £14,280 to successive restorations of St Margaret's during the period.[51]

Wyatt's estimates in 1807 for the restoration of the Henry VII Chapel were just over £25,000: £14,800 for the repairs and £10,400 for the ornamental parts. That the final cost was just under double the estimate must have come as a relief to those public officials who had to deal with Wyatt's somewhat casual attitudes to business. That the result in terms of architectural conservation was such a success must have been a more general surprise, especially to those, like the antiquary John Carter, who considered Wyatt the 'Great Destroyer' of medieval architecture. The answer seems to have been that with Wyatt removed by pressure of business and ill-health (he died in 1812) from the immediate supervision of the work, matters were carried on by the fruitful collaboration of two men. One was the Dean, John Vincent, who struggled to ensure that the restoration tackled all aspects of the building and its rich sculpted decoration in particular, rather than limiting the work to the minimum necessary for the survival of the structure. Although some have claimed that this led to the unnecessary removal of sound original stone, the evidence of the present restoration shows that much was retained, especially on the north side. The other member of the team was Thomas Gayfere, successor to his father as Master Mason of the Abbey, who was in charge of the programme as it developed on the ground. Gayfere took enormous pains in trying to achieve the best solutions, whether by personally researching for the best variety of stone to be used or by taking casts of the mouldings and other decayed architectural details. Meticulous measured drawings (later published) made by the architect J. N. Cottingham recorded what existed and provided authority for what had to be replaced. Their pains were rewarded by the welcome given to the restoration, both in their time and thereafter. Despite criticism of the parapets and cresting devised by Wyatt in place of the originals which had decayed entirely away, it has been recognized that the body of the chapel was intelligently treated, surviving subsequent pollution and war damage remarkably well.

The restoration was efficiently organized and recorded. The turrets were repaired in sequence starting at the south-east and alternating between south and north sides, and the parapets were rebuilt in a clockwise direction, beginning on the north side. The major alteration—apart from the rebuilding of the parapets and pinnacles—was over the western stair turrets. The decayed remains of what apparently had been lead-covered ogee domes were first removed for safety in 1803 and then replaced by large octagonal stone cupolas in 1822, in imitation of those over the turrets around the apse.

The deliberations concerning the choice of stone for the restoration were, for once, not confined to the Surveyor and the Chapter, but were conducted in the more public forum of the 'Committee for the Inspection of National Monuments,' commonly known as the Committee of Taste. This precursor of the Royal Fine Arts Commission included eminent connoisseurs such as Thomas Hope, Richard Payne Knight and Sir George Beaumont as well as leading artists such as John Flaxman and Richard Westmacott. The Henry VII Chapel, like the rest of the Abbey, was constructed of different types of stone: Reigate, Caen, Magnesian Limestone and Kentish Rag. Already in the late seventeenth century, Wren had noticed how badly the stones had reacted to London conditions and had therefore preferred to use Oxfordshire stone for his refacing. Hawksmoor employed Portland for all his work on the West Front, following the wisdom of his age that this was the stone best adapted to withstand the air pollution in the capital. Although Gayfere carefully explained these alternatives to the Committee, their choice was either Tottenhoe stone or Bath. For the former, Gayfere was instructed to inspect the performance of the masonry at St Alban's Abbey and at Woburn. In the event, he ultimately selected Bath stone quarried from Combe Down by Messrs Pierce.

35. The Henry VII Chapel. Engraving, *c.* 1740

36. View across lantern from South Transept, showing trompe l'oeil painting in lantern. Engraving, 1793

As always, the choice must have been influenced by considerations of aesthetics and cost, as well as durability. With the new canal system, Bath stone could be brought cheaply from the West Country to London. Its fine grain also made it well suited for the wealth of carved detail needed. Above all, its uniform colour, though not blending with the earlier Caen or Reigate, must have appealed to contemporary taste as suitable for a venerable religious building. At around this same time, William Wilkins treated the whole interior of Norwich Cathedral with a wash of this tint, deliberately removing the brightness of earlier polychromy in favour of a consistent tone.[52]

To digress from strict chronology, both nineteenth- and twentieth-century surveyors have found themselves in similar difficulties when having to choose the best stone to use. In 1840, Edward Blore considered Bath, Portland and also Caen stone for the proposed repairs on the North Transept. Caen was finally chosen, even though the mason, Samuel Cundy, priced it at £2 10s. a foot—5s. more than Bath stone.[53] An application from the Westminster Chapter to the Government in 1845

60

37. View of the nave, 1793,
by Thomas Malton

38. Presbytery, looking west, without furnishings,
showing Wyatt's lantern ceiling, *c.* 1819

asking for relief from import dues on the stone explains their reasoning: for the repairs of 1840–44 they had thought it advisable 'to use stone from Caen in Normandy' since the stone was not only 'peculiarly durable' but it was also 'the original stone from which the Abbey was built, harmonizing completely with the older work.'[54] Although much employed during this period for new work as well as for restoration (for instance at St Giles', Camberwell), this nineteenth-century Caen stone turned out to be much less durable than its medieval counterpart: thirty years later it was already known to be totally unsuitable.[55] Scott and his successor, John Loughborough Pearson, preferred Chilmark or Tisbury stone (used to build Salisbury Cathedral in the thirteenth century) since it was both longer-lasting and had a more suitable colour.[56] Both men censured Wren severely for his choice of Oxfordshire stone; yet restorations since the Second World War have found their solution to have been just as unsuccessful. (Only their use of Devonshire or, on the North Front, Kilkenny marble to replace Purbeck on the exterior has stood the test of time better.)

39. North side of Abbey
showing condition of masonry.
Engraving, *c.* 1800

The other significant event for the fabric of the Abbey during the early nineteenth century was the Coronation of George IV in 1821. Its notorious extravagance entailed costly alterations to the interior. The most conspicuous victim was the Queen Anne reredos, which had to be dismantled to provide a vast raking gallery to be built eastwards over the Shrine of St Edward. Before the coronation had even taken place, it was decided not to put the reredos back but to dispose of its various parts by gift or sale (Cat. no. 29). After the scaffolding erected for the ceremony had been dismantled and the Abbey reopened for public worship in March 1822, the Dean and Chapter had to decide what should be the proper treatment of the Sanctuary. The flanking monuments were now exposed to view, not concealed by hangings, as in the seventeenth century and possibly before or by the later wooden panelling 'of ill-designed and unmeaning carpentry.'[57]

This heightened awareness of the beauty of medieval monuments led to solutions which were abhorrent to Gothic revivalists of the later nineteenth-century. The 'Sebert monument,' or Sedilia, was drastically restructured so that the canopies were raised fourteen inches over a core of brickwork and cement. It was also decided not to insert a new design for the altar screen but to refashion the fifteenth-century one. Since the canopy work on the west face had been cut back to accommodate the Queen Anne reredos, it was necessary to renew these features. The Abbey authorities and their Surveyor, Benjamin Dean Wyatt, turned to the fashionable sculptor and stuccador Francis Bernasconi to reproduce these in plaster, a decision already attacked in 1843 as 'parsimonious.'[58] It must be stressed, however, that this was by no means a cheap job since the estimate accepted for it in 1823 was a costly £4,200. Because of the work he had previously carried out at York Minster, Southwell Minster and at the Galilee Porch in Ely Cathedral, Bernasconi was highly regarded for his ability to reproduce Gothic details accurately, whether in plaster or composition. To an age which saw no harm in using new, un-traditional materials in churches, as well as in houses or factories, his choice of plaster seemed sensible for this type of intricate work.

It was decided, perhaps by Bernasconi or by his employers, to continue the canopies straight across the screen rather than to observe the archaeological evidence of a rectangular panel behind the altar and thus to standardize the design of each canopy instead of repeating the original variation between them. This decision was again not due to poverty of finance or imagination, but to the preference of the period for uniformity. The texture and colour, 'the exact tint of unbaked pastry,' were chosen for the same aesthetic reasons as had led to the use of Bath stone in the Henry VII Chapel twenty years earlier.

40. B. D. Wyatt's design for an altar screen

41. The Coronation of Queen Victoria, June 28, 1838

IV · The Victorian Era

T HE VICTORIAN ERA left a great imprint on Westminster Abbey—as indeed it did everywhere. Much of the external masonry was refaced. The buttresses and pinnacles were taken down and reconstructed following different designs but allegedly closer to the original. The decorative crenellations around the whole church, depicted by Hollar and renewed by Wren, were replaced by Edward Blore with a continuous parapet which had a solid upper rail over continuous quatrefoils. The gable and upper parts of the North Transept were rebuilt in around 1840 and those of the whole South Transept thirty years later, with the plain walling being transformed into elaborate plate tracery. Some time later, the whole North Front—the pride of William Dickinson and Dean Atterbury[1]—was stripped away and redesigned by George Gilbert Scott and John Loughborough Pearson from the portals up to the gable. The Chapter House was equally transfigured by Scott, its utilitarian guise as a state record office changed back into a major work of art. Within the Abbey, every surface was treated over the years with a process of strengthening or 'induration' by injecting into the masonry 'a weak solution of white shellac in spirits of wine.'[2] The intention to secure and harden the crumbling stonework was successfully achieved; but the tonality of the Abbey interior was changed from silvery-grey to a brownish tinge. In terms of furnishings, a new set of stalls and a pulpit were introduced into the choir; another massive pulpit was brought into the nave; and stained glass was inserted in most of the windows in the building. The altar screen was restored and richly embellished with mosaic and marble. In the first years of the present century, altars in the side chapels and their associated furnishings began to be reinstated in their pre-Reformation locations, a process which gathered force over the succeeding years. Contemporary technology allowed the introduction of heating by a vast system of hot-water pipes, a revolution in terms of both human comfort and the preservation of the building, now spared the extremes of cold and damp. Photographs of about 1900 show the building complete with railings and gas lighting, both inside and out—the very model of a Victorian monument.

This picture is, however, misleading. Westminster Abbey did not experience the kind of comprehensive restoration which befell other great churches. There was no wholesale replacement of one style of Gothic by another more 'correct' one, even on the West Front and its Georgian 'Gothick' towers. The external profile of the building was little altered, except for the new steep-pitched roof of the Chapter House and its tall surrounding pinnacles.[3]

42. The North Front, as redesigned by Scott and Pearson. Photograph taken *c.* 1890

43. Choir, looking east, with Bernasconi's treatment of the altar screen. Photograph taken *c.* 1860

Scott, though elsewhere a vigorous and prolific designer, had limited impact on the fabric and furnishings of the Abbey. In his contemporary restorations at Ely and Salisbury, he was able to clear away all the eighteenth-century contributions made by James Essex and James Wyatt respectively. At Westminster, on the other hand, he reluctantly had to spend time and money in the 1850s reinstating the 'barbarous pinnacles of the West Towers,' built by Hawksmoor just over a century earlier.[4] In the choir, the furnishings installed by Blore in the 1840s have survived until the present day. Their style and general character stand out in clear contrast to the more elaborate and richly textured choir furnishings Scott provided for the cathedrals at Lichfield and Worcester twenty or thirty years later. Blore employed a more complex and archaeologically accurate version of the Gothic style than Keene had when the latter designed the previous stalls in the 1770s; but Blore chose to keep the surface treatment plain. He had 'no idea of varnishing or oiling the oak…Nothing was better than the colour as it looks now.'[5] The pieces exhibited (Cat. no. 42) present a more authentic picture of Blore's intentions than the stalls seen in the Abbey today, since these were gilded between the two World Wars by Sir Walter Tapper and then enlivened by Stephen Dykes Bower in the 1960s with a comprehensive colouring scheme.

The contrasts between the three Victorian Surveyors—Blore, Scott and Pearson—reveal much about changing public views concerning the restoration of historic buildings and the proper conduct of the liturgy as well as about their different personalities, techniques and attitudes towards the various aspects of their task. Blore is today the least well-known of the three men, despite the enormous scale of his architectural practice during the 1820s, 30s and 40s. Fortunately, a great deal of documentary material has been preserved in the Abbey Library, presumably given some time after his death. His drawings were likewise bequeathed to the Victoria & Albert Museum. The Abbey papers show the many haphazard problems which beset a surveyor, even today: questions of structural repairs appear mixed with arrangements for coronations or music festivals, and official reports to the Chapter are thrown in together with scribbled notes from deans, widows and workmen.

Attitudes in both the architectural and ecclesiastical worlds were changing rapidly during Blore's surveyorship. He occupied a transitional position. A good example is the question of the erection of monuments within the Abbey. This was a matter to which Blore had to dedicate much time and attention, whether dealing with requests by grandees for major monuments to public figures—like Lord Holland—or with less elevated pleas or complaints concerning their placing. Mrs Dudley North was determined that the monument to her husband, a political crony of Fox, should 'be judiciously—i.e. prominently—placed' and, though anxious 'to avoid any presumption of selecting too prominent' a site, refused the location offered below the belfry.[6] The sculptor Richard Westmacott considered he had 'certainly been very unfortunate hitherto in the situations assigned to my works in

XV. Detail of St John from a study for Stained Glass by Sir James Thornhill, *c.* 1720
Church of St Andrew, Chinnor [**28**]

XVI and XVII *(above)*. Front and back view of Cope made for the Coronation of Charles II, 1660–1661 **[18]**
XVIII and XIX *(below)*. Front and back view of Cope made for the Coronation of Edward VII, 1902 **[39]**

XX (right). Processional Banner designed by Sir Ninian Commper, 1922 **[40]**

the Abbey' and begged for better treatment.[7] Blore was no doubt vexed on occasion, but he does not seem to have questioned the practice itself. He was willing to promote a rationalization of it and offered a solution which, had it been accepted, would have proved more destructive to the architectural impression of the church than the addition of more free-standing monuments. His proposal was to provide additional space for memorials by lining the splays of the aisle windows with tablets of uniform size and shape, two, placed one on top of the other, on each side. The canopies were to be 'designed in a style to harmonize with the architecture of the church.'[8] The petitioner for the monument was 'to bear the expense of the canopy' and 'the architectural part of the work' would be executed by the Abbey Mason.[9]

From a utilitarian point of view, there was much to commend the idea. It would indeed have saved space, time and irritation. It would also have created a uniform neatness in place of the traditional confusion of monuments of different types, shapes, sizes and materials. Yet it is not hard to see why Scott rejected the whole idea as soon as he was appointed Surveyor in 1849. He opposed the introduction of 'a new architectural feature…and one by no means pleasing or consistent' with the original design of the church.[10] Moreover, by the 1840s advanced ecclesiastical thought was opposed to the practice of erecting in churches funerary monuments

44. Monuments along the north aisle. Engraving, 1812

45. Monument to Admiral Tyrrell,
original condition *c.* 1815

which celebrated personal achievements or social position rather than Christian doctrine.[11] Furthermore, there was a growing resistance based on architectural and archaeological grounds to adding more furnishings to the extraneous objects which had already been introduced in the Abbey or, as Scott put it, to increase the number of 'disfigurements which have already done so much to mar the effect of the church.'[12] Lining the aisle windows with modern tablets would have further diminished the effect of Westminster as a Gothic shrine. The trimmings in Gothic style proposed by Blore would have only added insult to injury.

From the mid century onwards, there was a move to reduce the number of monuments in the Abbey. For this, two steps were taken. The first was to become much more restrictive in the admission of new applications. Even Dean Stanley, fascinated with the famous and not so famous buried within the Abbey, approved the placing of only nine monuments in almost twenty years. The other step was to trim the modern monuments and their surroundings of their excess marble. Scott, who was at first opposed to the idea, commented in his last report on the process by which 'without the loss of any important features or any interesting associations, the architecture of the church has been brought more fully into sight and views obtained through arches formerly blocked.' The alterations were 'very ably arranged by Mr Poole acting under the direction of the dean and with very frequent consultations' with the Surveyor.[13] More was done in this way during Scott's time—and indeed well into this century—than is often recognized.[14] A comparison of the early nineteenth-century views by Ackermann with the present situation makes this point clear, especially in the nave aisles. For instance, in the monument of Admiral Tyrrell in the south aisle, the figure of the Admiral and the marble clouds surrounding him have been cut away to expose the window above.

46. Monument to Admiral Tyrrell, present state

The third solution proposed for the problem of 'surplus' monuments was the creation of a *Campo Santo* outside the Abbey that would receive existing memorials regarded as either too big or too unsuitable, as well as new commissions. Projects for such a national mausoleum continued to be put forward until the end of the century and some startling designs were prepared. As early as 1853, the sub-Dean, Lord John Thynne, had asked Scott to design a great memorial cloister running south from the Chapter House. Scott elaborated the idea ten years later, but the costs involved made the scheme impracticable, especially under the straitened circumstances of the Chapter at the time. Discussions began again in the 1880s, when such a memorial cloister was considered as a suitable memorial to Queen Victoria's Golden Jubilee in 1887. The ensuing controversy culminated in the setting up of a Royal Commission which reported in 1890. Pearson proposed impressive designs for both a site to the north of the nave and, like Scott, for the area around the Chapter House. The Commission preferred an alternative scheme which would transform the monastic refectory, now roofless and used as a garden, into a 'monumental chapel.'[15] Parliament was, however, not to be tempted. In the twentieth century, Edwin Maufe proposed a memorial cloister at the west end—with an equal lack of success.

Scott adopted a more professional and academic approach than Blore to the post of Surveyor. He made his annual reports regular and informative, distinguishing clearly between work that was desirable and work that was essential. On his appointment in March 1827, Blore had drafted out certain 'conditions' by which he intended to work.[16] Setting out lines of responsibility to control what was bought and what was ordered, these 'conditions', he stated, were chiefly designed to 'protect the Dean and Chapter against dishonesty or mismanagement'. From the start of his surveyorship, Scott adopted a more strategic and all-embracing approach, not only recommending immediate repairs but planning far into the future.

Scott considered his work at Westminster a 'great and lasting source of delight.'[17] He carried on his close involvement to the time of his death and imagined himself in his retirement still attending the daily service and wandering about 'the dear old place.'[18] He was clearly sincere when he wrote of the pleasure he felt in scrambling about the recesses of the Chapter House in the 1850s, finding 'lengths of the moulded ribs of the lost vaulting, carefully packed like wine bottles in a bin,' or letting down into a recess 'a small bull's-eye lantern' on a string which revealed 'the head of a beautiful full-sized statue in a niche.'[19] Twenty years later, Scott recorded after his break-down in 1870 that 'the very first day that I returned to business after my illness I went at once to the Abbey and for a time repeated my visits almost every day I went to town...climbing up high ladders, long before I had a right to do so and the work in respect of the research I have gone through (on the South Transept) is more than could well be imagined.'[20] In poignant contrast, Blore insisted on laying down the surveyorship after a mere twenty-two years and implied in his letter to

47. South Transept and Chapter House before restoration. Photograph taken *c.* 1860

48. The Chapter House under restoration. Photograph taken *c.* 1865–70

Thynne that he had been long thinking of it. Blore's retirement in favour of Scott was greeted by the campaigning High Church journal, the *Ecclesiologist*, 'with extreme satisfaction…We wish that the change had taken place sooner.'[21] When Scott died in office, he was honoured with a grand funeral in the Abbey. Ironically, the papers at Westminster suggest that Blore may have enjoyed a more personal rapport with the Abbey dignitaries. Scott consulted closely with both Dean Buckland and Dean Stanley and considered Lord Thynne, 'among my best friends.'[22] But there is nothing in the documents to match Dean Ireland's note to Blore: 'My dear Sir, I request you to call as soon as you can. In much hurry and distress of mind, I am yours…Tuesday night 28 April 1829.'[23]

Further contrasts stand out between Blore, Scott and Pearson relating to their theories of restoration. Blore's specification of 1836 for the repair of four windows is a mixture of radical and conservationist thinking. The window openings were to be in new Harley Down stone and the capitals and bases of the jamb shafts were to be replaced. Yet he stressed that all detailing must 'correspond exactly' with the existing design.[24] Similarly, when he noticed that the gable of the North Transept was unsafe, Blore set about its repair, changing perhaps some details but not redesigning it. When Scott, in turn, tackled the same part of the building, he was unwilling to repair the stonework of the eighteenth century and even that of Blore's period since the whole design was so inadequate: 'architecturally they are simply worthless.'[25]

Unlike Blore, Scott and Pearson tackled the complex questions of restoration with confidence, indeed with virtual certainty. Scott had a profound knowledge of medieval buildings, both in Britain and abroad. He had no qualms about getting his hands and clothes dirty rummaging in cupboards in search of concealed sculpture and architectural features, or climbing the scaffolding to peer behind the parapets. His researches on the Chapter House, even before the presses and panelling of the Record Office were stripped out, have already been mentioned.[26] With the Confessor's Shrine and the tomb of Queen Philippa (1328–69), he engaged in similar detective work, unearthing lost fragments and working out where they belonged. This involved not only archaeological skills, but also the imagination which allowed him to recognize pieces extracted from Queen Philippa's monument on the mantlepiece of Mr Cottingham's collection.

On those occasions when there was conflicting evidence, Scott stated his conviction that he had definitely reached the right conclusion. Commenting in 1868 on the restoration of two bays in the north walk of the cloister, he pointed out that 'these have been carried out with great exactness and may be confidently said to be a *precise* restoration of the original to its minutest details.'[27] The form of the base mouldings had been recovered by excavation, and that of the cusping from contemporary windows in the south aisle. Similarly, the detailing of the restored east portal of the North Front had been established by careful study of the evidence both before and during the works and by reference to 'other parts of the Abbey,' so that 'the result may be viewed as a trustworthy recovery of the old design.'[28] Pearson adopted the same tone when he described his refacing of the south side of the nave and aisles. He discovered 'most clearly marked' the original treatment of the clerestory windows, nave buttresses and aisles.[29] Not for them the honest perplexity expressed by Sydney Smirke in 1857 at Lichfield Cathedral when faced with the confused remains of the fourteenth-century alterations to the thirteenth-century choir: 'I believe I see what that treatment was but as long as there is uncertainty I feel uneasy in proceeding [with the restoration].' [30]

Scott reacted in a similarly confident fashion when there was criticism of his process of 'induration' by the use of shellac. He stated firmly in 1876 that 'it has been the saving of the Abbey.'[31] However, the cleaning programme carried out by Stephen Dykes Bower in the 1950s showed that it was possible to wash off the shellac without any signs of flaking being revealed in the original stonework underneath.[32]

Even Scott's diligent and imaginative scholarship could not preclude the discovery of new evidence which might contradict his first thoughts. The high altar screen was to have had a row of continuous canopied niches—following Bernasconi's reconstruction—but on stripping away the plaster it was discovered that instead of the central five niches there had originally been a plain rectangular recess.[33] More disturbing was John Oldrid Scott's admission, after his father's death, that the restoration design for the west portal of the North Front needed to be revised because the discovery of 'an encroaching projection' suggested that there should be an additional order of shafts. Since the shafts alone 'would have a poor effect' and were 'not likely' to have formed the original composition, they should be enriched with statues.[34] It is hardly surprising that the Abbey authorities did not continue to employ the young Scott and his brother.

Much more controversial than either of these episodes was Pearson's restoration of the North Front, from the portals up to the gable. Not content with replacing the Wren and Dickinson masonry, Pearson redesigned the major features. The tracery of the rose window was altered, with the radiating lights reduced in proportion (so cropping the feet of the eighteenth-century stained glass Apostles) and the pierced spandrels were filled. The tracery panelling of the gable was also altered and the crowning pinnacle replaced by a gable cross. The work was immediately denounced by William Morris as 'architect's architecture, the work of the office' which had damaged the exterior of the Abbey 'so vitally that scarcely any of its original surface remained.'[35] So great was the revulsion, that Lethaby (Pearson's eventual successor as Surveyor of the Abbey) could describe Pearson's restoration of the North Front in print only twenty years later as having 'made all false.'[36]

A century later, it is easier to see how Scott and Pearson could be sincere and usually successful in their claims to archaeological accuracy and yet also be criticized by their more conservation-minded successors. The evidence for the medieval

49. Scaffolding on the North Front.
Photograph taken *c*. 1887

50. North Front portal restored as by Scott,
but upper parts still by Dickinson. Photograph taken *c*. 1880

altar screen may have been accurately identified, but the end result, with the reredos of Salviati mosaic, the carvings by Armstead and the rich marbles and woodwork, tells of the 1860s, not of the fifteenth century. The conical roof and tall pinnacles of the Chapter House, virtually the only invention Scott added to his restoration, marked the whole building as Victorian. It is no discredit that even the restoration of Queen Philippa's monument, meticulously prepared by Scott and his most trusted craftsmen (Cat. no. 46), could reproduce the forms of the fourteenth-century designer only in the spirit of their own day.

Equally characteristic of their time were the patrons of the Victorian restorations, the successive Deans of Westminster. However, their broad interests rarely included architecture. The most famous, Arthur Penrhyn Stanley (Cat. no. 43) was passionately involved with the building, producing within a few years of his appointment *Historical Memorials of Westminster*, a classic account of the story and personalities of Westminster Abbey. He freely admitted to three surprising gaps in his qualifications as a Dean: no ear for music; 'ignorance of finance and incapacity for business;' and a 'want of architectural knowledge.'[37] Eminently successful in his efforts to make the Abbey 'more and more the centre for religious and national life in a truly liberal spirit,'[38] Stanley had no ambitions to refashion the outward expressions or furniture of worship. The symbolism of the new statues on the altar screen, Moses turning towards the statesmen commemorated in the North Transept and David looking south towards Poets' Corner, was 'Stanley's one piece of ritualism.'[39]

The most significant member of the Chapter in terms of care for the fabric was Lord Thynne, sub-Dean from 1831 to his death fifty years later. Though of a calibre to act as dean during Buckland's last years and even to be offered the post himself, Thynne preferred to act as a masterly second-in-command. Until his unofficial retirement in 1867, he was the first point of contact for a surveyor on matters of both business and aesthetics. As Scott tactfully expressed it, 'with all possible respect for the different members of the Chapter, I shall never feel that any of them possess the same judgement and powers of correct decision [as Thynne].'[40] Thynne's intelligent conservatism was, together with Stanley's disinterest in ecclesiology and the general lack of funds, a major factor in preserving the Abbey from wholesale renovation.

In fact, when put into the context of successive generations of work at Westminster, the nineteenth-century restorations do not seem so exceptional. The three major architects involved—Blore, Scott and Pearson—all had to work in ways familiar to their eighteenth-century predecessors: juggling important long-term issues relating to the fabric with the immediate requirements of the Dean and Chapter, and operating within a constrained budget.

The funds available diminished rather than increased. When the Ecclesiastical Commissioners sequestered in 1869 a large proportion of the historic endowment of the Abbey for distribution elsewhere, they calculated that the landed estates

51. Detail from the proposed restoration of Queen Philippa's tomb. Victoria and Albert Museum, London

remaining in the hands of the Chapter would go on producing enough to support both the canons and the maintenance of the services and fabric. The sum of £20,000 per annum was the figure agreed, with a further £20,000 assigned as a capital sum to cover 'essential repairs' of the Abbey and other buildings.[41] Unfortunately, the agricultural depression almost immediately overturned those assumptions. By 1880, the arrears due from stricken tenants were several times greater than the slender credit balance of the Chapter. Even during the time that later generations consider the golden years of the nation's late Victorian prosperity, Pearson had to plead against a sudden stop of work on the North Transept.[42] To have taken down the scaffolding at that moment would have cut off the programme at a most damaging stage and incurred the added costs of the removal of the scaffolding and making good of the exposed masonry. Scott took care to present to the Dean and Chapter each year a modest list of recommended projects, while reminding them from time to time that a more extensive programme could not be delayed indefinitely. As early as 1854, he urged that 'on whatever portion of the fabric it may be preferred to direct our operations, no year may be permitted to pass without some substantial work of reinstatement.'[43] Yet ten years later 'scarcely anything' had been done. Scott had to take 'the liberty of recalling your [the Dean and Chapter's] attention to the vast amount of work of a very pressing nature which has to be done and to the very *small* amount of work annually effected.'[44]

Until the commutation of the estates in 1869, the Dean and Chapter's sources of finance remained similar to those of the eighteenth century. These came partly from land and partly from the fees collected from visitors and those chargeable for burials and memorials.[45] The latter declined during the century—as did the estate income— owing to a growing reluctance to compromise the religious 'tone', whether by charging for admission or by filling the building with yet more memorials. The total fee for viewing the Abbey, which in the early nineteenth century had risen as high as 2s., was reduced in 1825 by public pressure to 1s. 3d. In 1841 the principle of free admission was granted, though there were still fees for viewing the nave, the North Transept, and the Royal Chapels. Dean Stanley granted free entry on every Monday of the year and bequeathed £3,000 to allow the same privilege on Tuesdays.[46] Thus, much of the £1,500–£2,000 earned from fees in the 1820s was high-mindedly foregone, although the costs of providing vergers to patrol and clean the building still remained.[47]

The aesthetic arguments against installing more monuments have already been discussed.[48] In terms of finance, fewer monuments and burials meant less money for fabric repairs. Whereas there were eighteen monuments erected and twenty-three burials between 1827 and 1836, there were only two monuments placed and eleven burials between 1856 and 1865.[49] Since the fee for installing a full-scale monument could amount to £200, the loss of income was therefore considerable.

The Dean and Chapter had to look outside for financial aid. The Parliamentary grants which had financed both the Wren and the Wyatt restorations were no longer forthcoming. Government help was sought in 1886 in connection with the restoration of the North Transept. The resulting Westminster Abbey Act of 1888 solved the problem, not by giving public funds, but by altering the Abbey's arrangements with the Ecclesiastical Commissioners. The Government did put money aside for the repair of the royal tombs in the 1850s, though in the event little was used. It also paid for the restoration of the Chapter House between 1868 and 1873 after the removal thence of the Public Records, but only because the Chapter House had been—and remained—the property of the State not of the Chapter.

For the substantial funds necessary to launch major works, the Dean and Chapter had to look to the Ecclesiastical Commissioners and their capital of £20,000 committed to the restoration of the fabric. Even such an experienced cathedral architect as Scott had to admit in 1871 that 'it was a difficult task to recommend the exact course to be pursued during the present year because my mind is somewhat confused between the different funds from which we have to draw.'[50] In that particular case, Scott reckoned that the Fabric Fund could bear the continuing programmes of re-leading the roofs and of 'induration' of the stonework; but the grant from the Ecclesiastical Commissioners and the interest earned on it should cover 'the most pressing works.'[51] However, in a letter to Thynne only three days before, Scott had admitted that 'the sum seems insufficient for the pressing needs of a building of

52. Masons' shop during the restoration of the North Transept. Photograph taken 1889

such vast magnitude.'[52] Hence the anxiety at Westminster Abbey, as for instance at Norwich Cathedral at the same time, to obtain the interest and support of Ewan Christian, the official architect of the Ecclesiastical Commissioners, when any major scheme of repair was in prospect. Nearly twenty years later, Pearson reported that he had discussed 'the most important matters' with Ewan Christian, who had surveyed the Abbey for the Commissioners, and stated that 'Christian entirely concurs...as to the state of the Abbey and the urgent necessity' for works of restoration.[53]

The problems produced by working in such constrained circumstances are vividly illustrated by what might seem to be a savage indictment of Scott's surveyorship of all but thirty years: the findings of Pearson's first full report of March 1882. The latter had discovered 'with much sorrow' that 'the masonry in many places' was 'in a far worse condition than I had anticipated' and had even become 'loose and unsafe.' His estimate for repairs, exclusive of the West Towers, was £49,000. The main target of Pearson's criticism was not Scott but Wren, for his choice of Oxfordshire or Portland stone and also for his use of iron cramps. Indeed, the Oxfordshire stone had decayed on the south side of the nave seven or eight inches behind Wren's surface.[54] Referring to the West Towers in 1896, Pearson commented that 'nothing indeed has surprised me more than this extensive use...of iron cramps and wedges if this work were done under Sir Christopher Wren's immediate superintendence for no one more fully realized than he had the injurious effect of them upon masonry.'[55]

The nineteenth-century surveyors, like their predecessors and successors, had to cope with the Dean and Chapter as both employers and tenants of the Abbey buildings. Their continuing domestic use by the canons and their families; by the other members of the Abbey establishment; and, not least, by the boys of Westminster School—the status of which was only distinguished from the Abbey in 1868—could lead to some curious situations. Scott complained of the tendency to fill underused spaces (such as the room he knew as the Chapel of St Blaize but now called by its original dedication to St Faith) with 'heterogeneous objects which from time to time accumulate in them.'[56] Even more reprehensible was the 'somewhat ludicrous and unseemly scene' presented by the triforium of the South Transept which acted as a 'depository of all the rejected water-closet apparatus and obsolete plumbers work from surrounding houses.'[57] Similar domestic problems still beset Pearson at the end of the century. The Clerk of Works, Thomas Wright, wanted storage space to keep carved stones and other objects of interest discovered during the many decades of nineteenth-century restoration. The only site available was a disused scullery in the Deanery.[58] At the same time, it was necessary to improve the lavatory outside Poets' Corner which was not only 'deficient from a sanitary point of view,' but could not 'supply the increased requirements since the police have been about the Abbey.'[59]

The cloisters had a dual role. They acted as a burial ground for those of lesser rank either associated with the Abbey during their careers, for instance musicians or masons, or, for those like George Vertue the engraver, who achieved a fame and station in life distinguished enough for recognition but not for burial within the Abbey walls. They also long remained the rough playground of the Westminster boys.[60] In the eighteenth century, the boys frightened off Horace Walpole from visiting the monument he had erected to his mother in the Henry VII Chapel and persecuted the young William Blake. As late as 1847, they disturbed an impressive consecration of four colonial bishops with a bare-fisted boxing match fought in the cloister garth.[61] Others used the cloisters as a thoroughfare for journeys into the town through the Abbey. The boldly 'gothick' iron gates of 1721–2 (attributed to Dickinson) across the east and west walks were one solution to the problem but, not surprisingly, the condition of the cloisters became ever more dilapidated. Scott commented in 1866 that, although they retained 'more ancient material' than other parts of the exterior, they were 'getting into a very sad state.'[62] Repairs proved controversial, except for the lowering of the ground level of the garth by 3.5 feet in 1869–70. Scott insisted, as was noted above, that the renewal of the thirteenth-century bays in the north walk was done with great exactness, 'preserving all parts which it was possible to reuse.' Glazing was restored to the upper parts of the openings as 'agreeable in effect and helpful in stopping the rain beating across the cloister walks.'[63] Nevertheless, many felt that too much had been lost.

The Westminster establishment was imaginative in finding new ways to express the Abbey's central position in national life and reconcile its ceremonial role with pastoral innovation, notably by means of the introduction of regular services in the nave in 1858 and the special occasions devised by Dean Stanley. It remained, however, conservative both in liturgical practice and in liturgical furnishings. With the gradual establishment of a Tractarian ritual as the norm in Anglican life, there appeared to be a meanness in the setting forth of worship at Westminster, whether in objects such as vestments, frontals and plate, or in the arrangement and decoration of the Sanctuary and side-chapels. The 'sweetness and light' of the late nineteenth-century ecclesiologists came late to the Abbey. John Thomas Micklethwaite, Scott's pupil and later Surveyor of the Fabric, had apparently never 'come across a great church…so miserably equipped save in the one outstanding feature of plate.'[64] The modest rood cross he added to the Confessor's Shrine in 1902 when an altar was re-established in St Edward's Chapel (Cat. no. 38) caused great dissensions in the Chapter on its first appearance.[65] Yet such Catholic imagery soon passed without comment as the sacristy was refurnished over succeeding years with an almost medieval abundance of textiles, metal and woodwork (Cat. no. 39).

The exception which proves the rule regarding High Victorian indifference to furnishings at the Abbey was the refashioning of the altar screen. The time taken to accomplish the work, its cost, and the significance of the project were out of all

53. The High Altar, *c.* 1863

proportion to its size. The project was agreed in 1862–63, it was unveiled—unfinished—in Easter 1867 and eventually dedicated six years later. As has been mentioned earlier, archaeological evidence revealed midway was respected, and Scott had to enlarge the surround for the Salviati mosaic now discovered to be too small to fill the original recess. But there was no idea of reproducing a medieval iconography. The reredos depicts the Last Supper, derived by Clayton and Bell from Leonardo's mural, which was already established as an acceptable Protestant image. The scene is flanked by statues of Moses and David, again scriptural figures which recall the traditional Anglican pairing of Moses and Aaron at the altar. Moreover, the choice of rich materials carried a message of both material and spiritual empire. As Dean Stanley said in his dedication sermon, the alabaster and marble from

XX (right). Processional Banner designed by Sir Ninian Commper, 1922 **[40]**

Britain, and the mosaic, porphyry and other stones from abroad were combined 'in the service of Him who has given us the heathen for our possession, the uttermost parts of the earth for our inheritance.'[66]

There is no space to discuss in detail the contribution of the successive craftsmen who worked in the Abbey during the nineteenth century. While each surveyor had his favourites, he was as reliant on them as they were on him. A list—probably prepared by Thynn—of the sums totalling £22,041 paid to individual craftsmen and artists for internal works and embellishments over the years 1841–67 gives some 'league table' as to the relative size of the various contributions.[67] Francis Ruddle of Peterborough, the contractor favoured by Blore for his restorations at Peterborough and Norwich as well as at Westminster, came at the head. A total of nearly £6,000 was produced for his work first on the organ case, then on the choir involving the translation of Blore's wiry designs into durable and archaeologically correct wood-work (Cat. nos. 42 and 44). His work was generally reckoned at the time to be 'done very neatly,' although in the matter of the new organ case in 1834 Dean Ireland was most indignant at Ruddle's 'entire inattention to the principles by which woodwork is applied to the propagation of sound.'[68]

Also amongst the most-favoured builders was Scott's preferred contractor, the Abbey Master Mason, Henry Poole and his sons. They had a more broadly based business than Ruddle, taking on the repair and replacement of structural masonry as well as that of finely detailed furnishings. Scott put great reliance on them although his successor, Pearson, seems to have been less impressed. The latter noted in 1884 that 'on an estimate of £3,500, he had obtained prices…considerably lower than those I had when I first began the restoration of the Abbey.'[69]

In the more strictly decorative fields of stained glass, painting and mosaic, the standard names predominate: Ward and Nixon; Salviati; Clayton and Bell. In response to a query about the work of William Morris and Faulkner, Scott admitted that they were 'talented artists, rather of the "pre-Raphaelite" school,' but continued in a cautious tone, stating that 'tastes differ respecting their works, although they are pretty generally admitted to be men of superior talent…They are men of education and even I believe of some literary position.'[70] Not surprisingly, Morris and his firm contributed little to the Abbey, and neither did Burne-Jones and, a little later, the men of the Arts and Crafts Movement.

Though conservative in their choice of artist as well as in their taste in furnishings, the Abbey authorities did share the contemporary enthusiasm for stained glass. In 1840, Blore wrote a circular letter to a number of firms and individuals, such as Thomas Willement, with an established reputation in the field, inviting them on behalf of the Chapter to compete for glazing the windows in the south wall of the South Transept, including the great rose window.[71] They wished to give 'artists of our own country' the chance to produce work 'in no respect inferior to the boasted works of the Continental glass stainers and worthy of the building it is intended to

XXI. Westminster Abbey, Choir and Apse

embellish.' However, this positive attitude did not stretch to providing either fees or expenses to the competitors. The winners were Ward and Nixon who agreed, in December 1841, to glaze all the windows for a sum of £2,000.[72] Despite the chauvinistic tone of the competition, the glaziers were instructed to visit the 'finest specimens on the Continent, especially in Munich, Freibourg and Nuremberg' before beginning their work.

In contrast to the much better preservation of the medieval fragments and even of the eighteenth-century glass, nothing survives of Ward and Nixon's scheme; and very little is left of the many windows inserted during the next sixty years. The loss was partly caused by bomb damage and partly by the determined efforts in the twentieth century to exchange the vivid but dark colours of the Victorian era for a cooler, more translucent style based on late medieval examples. Typical of this change of taste is the set of royal benefactors filling the north aisle windows of the nave, begun by Sir Ninian Comper in 1907 but installed over the next forty years.

54. Corbel from the memorial bust of Charles Kingsley, by Thomas Woolner [47]

V · The Twentieth Century

by Donald Buttress

B Y THE YEAR 1900, the great age of ecclesiastical restoration was almost over. Much had been achieved at the Abbey during the past sixty years by Blore, Scott and Pearson. The North Transept had been vigorously repaired and recast. Less had been carried out on the South Transept, but it now had more elegant and appropriate upper parts. The buttresses and flyers of the nave, choir and transepts had been put in order, and the Chapter House, although still in Crown hands, had been reconstructed inside and out according to what Scott thought had been its original form.

Little work had been done on the Henry VII Chapel, not surprisingly since it had been thoroughly refaced less than a century before, and even less had been done to the West Front. The men of Scott's generation would have preferred to reface the two towers in a more appropriate form, removing the mixture of classical and Gothic elements and introducing authentic detailing. Had work been carried out on the towers, the front might have emerged more like, for example, the rebuilt twin towers of Selby Abbey or Bridlington Priory, both carried out by John Oldrid Scott, who, significantly, did not succeed his father as Surveyor of Westminster Abbey.

When Pearson died in 1897, there was no obvious successor to the surveyorship. The generation of Street and Butterfield were all gone and Bodley was by now an old man. Younger architects like Temple Moore and Comper were still rising stars. John Thomas Micklethwaite, a former pupil of Scott, was not the obvious choice; but his appointment as Surveyor in 1897 ensured the continuation of sound restoration although he instigated no spectacular developments. His appointment coincided with an age of self-confidence within the Church of England which expressed itself in the embellishment of many churches. At Westminster, these included the new altar, cross and pall which Micklethwaite installed in St Edward's Chapel in 1902 (Cat. no. 38)

The major work on the fabric was the repair of the West Front. At the north-west corner of the north tower, Micklethwaite seems to have replaced decayed fifteenth-century details as he found them, possibly removing some of the Hawksmoor detailing of panels and canopies but replacing as little as possible in order to save money. Micklethwaite used Portland stone in place of the original Caen, and adopted a full Perpendicular vocabulary for the canopy heads, crockets and mouldings, based on the mutilated details he found there already. The two huge frontal buttresses on either side of the west window he treated differently. The one on the

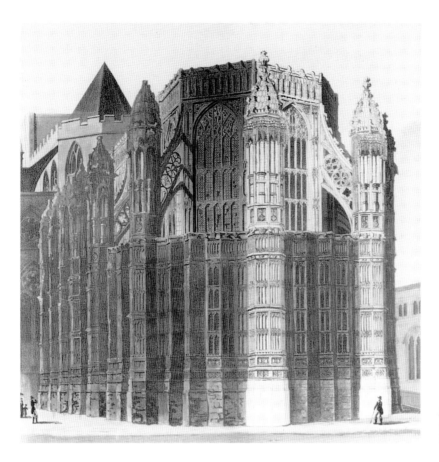

55. The Henry VII Chapel in 1811,
with two pinnacles restored.
Engraving

56. The Henry VII Chapel, from the north-east,
with restoration almost complete. Drawing by John Coney, 1816

57. Measured drawing showing decorative details on the Henry VII Chapel

south seems to have been little touched since its early eighteenth-century form was not altered. Presumably in 1900 its Portland stone was still in good condition. However, Micklethwaite seems to have rebuilt the north buttress in Chilmark stone with the same authentic Perpendicular features he had followed in the design of the canopies. It is uncertain whether Micklethwaite's restraint was caused by the shortage of money or whether it was because he had a different cast of mind from Scott and Pearson and was less interventionist in matters of design. He was the first of a new kind of surveyor: one mindful of the doctrines and censures of the Society for the Protection of Ancient Buildings, a body which had savaged poor Pearson in his latter years for his work at the Abbey and at Peterborough Cathedral.

William Richard Lethaby, appointed Surveyor after Micklethwaite's death in 1906, was even less inclined than his predecessor to make any changes. He treated the fabric with great respect and studied it with intense care, but he did not embark on delicate matters of design. In any case, the advent of the Depression and two World Wars made the first half of this century an inauspicious time for major undertakings. Paradoxically, the Abbey's place in popular affection as the centre of the Empire grew stronger during this time. It became the place for elaborate royal marriages, such as those of the Princess Royal and the Duke of York, and, most memorably, for the burial of the Unknown Warrior in 1920 at the west end of the nave. The latter is a curious illustration of what has so often been the case, that the noblest sentiments have found expression in an artifact of the most ordinary character. The quality of the brass lettering on the tablet is unexceptional, when it could so easily have been done by any one of a number of distinguished contemporary craftsmen. Eric Gill, for example, was in his prime.

Lethaby remained as Surveyor until 1928. His main memorials are the two books he wrote: *Westminster Abbey and the Kings' Craftsmen* and *Westminster Abbey Re-examined* published in 1906 and 1925 respectively. He was followed by Sir Walter Tapper, one of the best-known of the older generation of church architects. He soon became caught up in the controversy concerning the addition of a sacristy in the angle between the North Transept and the East End. Tapper and the Dean, William Foxley Norris, were firm advocates of the proposal, but they were eventually defeated by public opposition. He was more successful, however, with his proposed changes to the fabric. On his arrival, he awakened the Chapter to the realization that firm action was needed. Victorian repairs to the nave, which had, as noted earlier, used unsuitable Chilmark stone, were breaking down and giving cause for anxiety. But it was to the Henry VII Chapel that Tapper turned his immediate attention.

Recent internal scaffolding has revealed just how thorough his repairs to the intricate vaulting must have been. The interior was scaffolded in 1932 and the upper parts carefully examined, cleaned and secured. Small pieces had already fallen and there was clearly an anxiety about the stability of the rest. Tapper's repairs were of the most workmanlike kind. The pendants were secured by means of bronze

58. Bomb damage to the exterior of the Henry VII Chapel.
Photograph taken in October 1940

cramps, lead caulking, non-ferrous screws and bolts. Where individual stone seg-
ments of the vault had moved, they were secured as a precaution with iron and
bronze straps and with bars threaded through metal rings. Open masonry joints
between individual stones were raked out, packed with slate or lead, and soundly
repointed. The whole vault surface was limewashed, as were the walls and tracery
down to window level, the apsidal chapels and the north and south aisles. Finally,
at the foot of Henry VII's tomb, Tapper created a new altar and altar canopy, skilfully
incorporating fragments of Torrigiano's original design, which had survived the
altar's destruction and dispersal in the mid seventeenth century.

On the outside of the Chapel, Tapper found the cupolas in a state of advanced
decay. He repaired the tops of four of them on the south side—presumably those
in the worst condition—using Portland stone, but unfortunately not of the best
quality.

Tapper died in 1935 and the Dean and Chapter appointed Sir Charles Peers as
Surveyor, who was already over sixty years of age and had recently retired as Chief
Inspector of Ancient Monuments at the Ministry of Works. In effect, because of the
outbreak of the war in 1939, he became an able caretaker-occupant of the office,
supervising the removal of many valuable fittings to places of safety, the protection
of others *in situ* and their reinstatement at the end of hostilities.

During the war, a bomb pierced the roof of the crossing. It destroyed Wyatt's
ceiling, but otherwise did relatively little damage inside. Many stained glass windows were destroyed. Fortunately, those removed in 1939 or otherwise protected
were saved. The Chapel of Henry VII suffered considerable blast damage from at

59. Debris on the floor of the Choir and the damaged High Altar.
Photograph taken in May 1941

least one bomb in Old Palace Yard and further evidence of shrapnel has been discovered during the present restoration. The hole pierced through the east wall was not filled after the war, but was left as a glazed opening to testify to the damage. As in the rest of the Abbey, the stained glass was heavily damaged, including the remaining fragments of the original glazing.

The Deanery, the houses in the vicinity of the Little Cloister, and the buildings of Westminster School were severely damaged. The former dormitory, now the 'School' Room, was gutted. After the war, the rebuilding of the Deanery and the Canons' houses to a different scale and style to that of their predecessors was put in the hands of Seely and Paget, since Peers was elderly by then and out of main stream architectural practice.

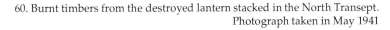

60. Burnt timbers from the destroyed lantern stacked in the North Transept.
Photograph taken in May 1941

The Coronation of 1953 once again focused worldwide attention on the Abbey. However, it was evident that considerable effort would have to be made on making repairs to the fabric which had suffered from war damage, neglect, and the inactivity caused by the Depression and war-time shortages. Apart from Tapper's work on the Henry VII Chapel, little had been done to the structure of the Abbey since the close of the previous century.

Stephen Dykes Bower had replaced Peers in 1951 and, two years later, an appeal for one million pounds was launched. With characteristic aplomb, Dykes Bower continued the internal cleaning of the church, begun before the war by Lethaby and continued by Tapper. During the 1960s, the interior of the church was transformed so that it could be appreciated in a way not seen since at least the seventeenth century, before the dirt of London had turned it quite literally soot black. The cleaning was a great success; as was the renewal of the glazing which involved replacing the Victorian glass damaged during the War with clear glass following Wren's patterns of lead and ferramenta. This is especially effective in the clerestories of the nave, choir and transepts, flooding the cleaned interior with light.

61. Interior of the Abbey prepared for the Coronation of Queen Elizabeth II

More controversial was Dykes Bower's treatment of the furnishings and monuments. The repair and spectacular repainting of the coloured decoration of the great architectural memorials of the Tudor and Jacobean periods are judged by many to be a success and the full colouring of the late medieval Bourchier memorial in the north ambulatory gives a present-day observer some idea of the splendour of medieval polychromy. However, the same richness applied to Blore's nineteenth-century west front of the pulpitum and to his choir stall canopies could be considered overdone. One of Dykes Bower's greatest achievements was to reinstate, with the help of his assistant Alan Rome, Pearson's magnificent organ cases which had been removed at the time of the 1937 Coronation. The removal of most of the brass candelabra light fittings (which now survive only in the Sanctuary) and their replacement by the huge silvery chandeliers of Irish Waterford glass, given by the Guinness family, have also been questioned. Further controversy arose towards the end of Dykes Bower's incumbency over a proposal—eventually abandoned—to re-pave the floor of the nave and transepts with a new design, rearranging the floor monuments in new locations.

The changes introduced by Dykes Bower on the fabric itself were effective in promoting its future stability. Blore's openwork parapets were replaced by crenellations, returning to a version of the medieval battlements devised by Wren and Hawksmoor. The timber roofs of the nave and transepts were completely reconstructed. Work was proceeding on those of the choir when outside opinion was roused by the realization that the surviving medieval trusses were being discarded. A dispute ensued, about which all the facts may never be clear. Suffice it to say that the Abbey now has well-constructed trusses and a superstructure soundly covered with new cast lead. It is however to be regretted that what survived of the old roofs was not recorded more thoroughly before removal.

In 1972, Marshall Sisson was called in to advise over the high roof controversy. After his early death and the retirement of Dykes Bower in 1973, Sisson's partner, John Peter Foster, was appointed sixteenth Surveyor of the Fabric that same year. By then, the one million pounds raised as a result of the 1953 appeal had been exhausted. A further effort was clearly required on the exterior in order to deal with the failure of the nineteenth-century repairs and tackle properly the repair of the West Front and the Henry VII Chapel. The Westminster Abbey Trust, under the Chairmanship of HRH Prince Philip, Duke of Edinburgh, set about to raise five million pounds. By 1995, twenty-five million pounds will have been raised and spent, including the one and a half million pounds raised by the Speaker's Appeal for St Margaret's Church, a sum equivalent to five million pounds in 1973 prices.

As has already been mentioned, various types of building stones are found on the exterior of the Abbey, each of which weathers differently. Surviving medieval Reigate stone on the north side of the nave shows that it can stand up to erosion quite well if used in plain ashlar blocks. However, it withstands erosion less well in exposed locations such as parapets and string courses. In the recent repairs of the medieval core of the West Towers, evidence found behind later facing material shows that the plain Reigate blocks of the wall were originally protected by harder Caen stone. Since the time of Micklethwaite, it had become standard practice to use Portland limestone for most repairs to the Abbey, mainly because of its ability to withstand the attack of London atmosphere—especially in exposed positions. However, its use for patchwork and scattered repairs has proved less successful since, in contrast to older stonework, they tend to be visually over-prominent, for instance, on the north side of the nave.

Cleaning and repair began on the north side of the nave in 1973 and continued eastwards rapidly, reaching the apsidal chapels by the end of the 1970s. Foster's greatest task in this area was the overhaul and repair of the North Transept, last dealt with a century before by Scott and Pearson. The Chilmark stone which they had used had deteriorated very badly and needed extensive replacement; and this meant the almost total rebuilding of the upper gable and pinnacles. This process is explained in Foster's pamphlet *Ten years of Restoration at Westminster Abbey* published by the Ecclesiological Society in 1985. He made no attempt to change the design, except to enlarge and improve the weatherings in order to resist the attack of the elements more effectively.

About 1980, financial considerations persuaded the Trustees and the Dean and Chapter to postpone work on the Henry VII Chapel, in favour of the more urgent task of repairing the South Transept and the south side of the nave. As on the north side, the upper parts of Scott's high south transept gable were almost totally replaced in Portland stone instead of the decayed Chilmark. Important new sculptures were carved by Arthur Ayres, assisted by Tim Metcalfe, notably the new Christ in Majesty below the gable cross which was subsequently awarded a special commendation by the Masons Company.

The condition of the south side of the nave, with its complex series of flying buttresses, had been the cause of growing concern since the 1930s. In the mid nineteenth century, Scott and Pearson had rebuilt the flyer arms and recased the buttress piers in Chilmark stone, removing the early eighteenth-century work but leaving much of the medieval core in place. By the mid 1980s, the condition of some flyer arms was critical, threatening the security of the nave vaults. During the Victorian repairs, certain details were changed, though exactly what and when are now hard to determine. The present appearance of the great buttress terminations is as left by Pearson and Scott since Foster made no significant changes. The design is hardly medieval and is probably the result of seventeenth-or early eighteenth-century simplification of the original pinnacles into obelisks, subsequently enriched by finials and foliage in the successive nineteenth-century restorations. Rebuilding the flyers on four levels, whilst maintaining the superincumbent weight of the pinnacles on which the stability of the structure partly depends, was a complex building and engineering task. With the help of the skills of David James of RJ James and Partners, a system of propping and strutting and a phased programme of renewal of each of the stone flyer arms were devised, so that the task could be carried out with minimum risk.

Once the south side of the nave was finished, two major projects remained to be tackled: first the West Front and later the Henry VII Chapel. By early 1989, the complex operation to restore the entire West Front had been carefully planned and costed at around six million pounds. After a period of investigation, a start was made that same year on the south west tower under the direction of a new Surveyor, Donald Buttress, appointed following Foster's retirement in 1988.

The first and very big task was the design of the scaffolding for the West Towers. To the south, it had to be carried above the lower buildings of the Deanery and the Jerusalem Chamber on a huge steel framework supported on piles. Over the west entrance, used by thousands of people on busy days, a huge projecting overhead gantry was essential. On the north side, the instability of the made-up ground—formerly occupied by vanished buildings—made it necessary to cast a concrete raft foundation bearing on some forty piles in order to give the scaffolding independent support.

The main problems found were damage to the external facing stone by rusting eighteenth-century lead-encased iron cramps and severe damage to the four main levels of overhanging cornices by iron corrosion and deep penetration by rainwater. At the highest level, it was found to be necessary to rebuild Hawksmoor's pierced parapets, replace two corner pinnacles completely, and repair the other six. The timber roofs of both towers were repaired and re-covered in lead.

Internally, both towers needed attention. In the south west tower, a huge wooden frame, made partly of medieval and Georgian timbers, was repaired so it could fulfil its vital function of providing internal bracing. In the north west tower, the steel bell frame of 1919 and other surviving timbers performed the same function. New glazing was inserted behind the louvres of the eight main belfry openings to exclude the weather; ventilation was carefully rearranged; and the soft internal stone surfaces were limewashed for better protection.

Externally, the northern buttress, nearly 90 feet high, was greatly decayed, even though it had been rebuilt less than a century ago in Chilmark stone. It was taken down and reconstructed in Portland stone, retaining some Victorian details but conforming in its general line with its matching southern neighbour on the other side of the window. There, Hawksmoor's more 'gothick' details, such as the profiles of the mouldings and the design of the upper pinnacles, were retained. The north-west angle of the north west tower was entirely replaced, using Portland stone on the north side and St Maxim limestone (matching medieval Caen) on the east side, where more of the old work remained. The drawing (ill. 62) shows the respective

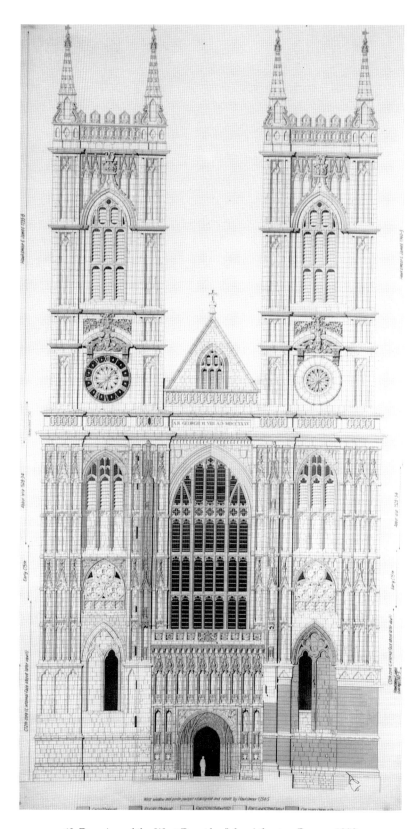

62. Drawing of the West Front by John Atherton-Bower, 1990

63. The West Front. Detail of photograph taken in 1993 by Anthony Osmond-Evans

areas of each main period of masonry now surviving on the western elevation. The lowest thirty feet of the north west tower had been given a thin and inadequate casing of Portland stone, enclosing the fifteenth-century Reigate. When it was removed—and before being more securely re-fixed and tied back with new cramps—the opportunity was taken to examine the old inner face. This revealed beyond any doubt that parts of the late Norman towers still existed, enclosed within first the fifteenth-century and then the eighteenth-century work.

Finally, attention turned to the area surrounding the western portal. This is still mainly a fifteenth-century work in magnesian limestone, except for the Portland stone used by Hawksmoor for his vigorous restorations of the niche canopies and his new classical cornice. Repairs were made in matching materials (Jackdaw Cragg) and protected by a renewed Portland cornice. Then the whole porch was lime-washed for the greater protection of this single most extensive area of surviving external medieval fabric.

Some additions to the West Front were made during this last restoration. A new high gable cross was added to a plinth dating from the eighteenth century; six new life-size statues in Richmont stone were placed in the niches of the two frontal buttresses; and an inscription was cut in the lowest part of the north west tower and unveiled by HRH Prince Philip to commemorate the completion of the work in March 1992. In 1994, alterations were made to the railings, obelisks and bollards surrounding the west end of the North Green in order to provide a larger open space for visitors and improve access. Openwork iron pylons and new gas lanterns have been added to the west gate piers.

Also at this time, repairs were made to the roof and parapets of the Jerusalem Chamber and Scott's crenellations were rebuilt in Portland stone. Coped termina-tions were added to Blore's former Chapter Office—now the Bookshop—based on those designed by G. F. Bodley for the porch of St Margaret's Church.

By 1993, the main focus of the restoration programme had passed to the Henry VII Chapel. As was described before, the last comprehensive restoration of the Chapel had taken place between 1809 and 1822, when the exterior was reclad in fine quality Combe Down stone. Evidence found during the present restoration suggests that a surprising amount of medieval Caen stone was retained, especially on the less exposed north side, including some window tracery and areas of wall panelling in sheltered places, such as the window jambs. Other ancient masonry was taken out, reversed and then reset. There is much evidence of the intricate piecing in of re-used smaller stones, probably done for reasons of economy as well as for any antiquarian reverence for the material itself. Smaller medieval fragments were re-used as rubble to fill the cores of the sixteen octagonal cupolas, which were all rebuilt.

The Trustees, undaunted by almost twenty years of fund-raising, eventually agreed to raise the five million pounds necessary to restore the Chapel. Even this huge sum envisaged the possible use of some cast artificial stone ornament, instead of natural stone for the more repetitive elements of the design. Eventually, this idea—although consistent with late Georgian practice (for example in the use of Coade stone)—was abandoned in favour of natural stone, which increased the approved budget to six million pounds. The Dean and Chapter made available an additional £200,000 for a programme of internal renovation, relighting and heating, and a repetition of Tapper's internal limewashing.

The first priority was to ensure overall structural stability by the reconstruction of the remaining twelve great cupola tops, each weighing over 10 tonnes and in an advanced state of decay. As was the case before their nineteenth-century restoration, they were losing much of the intricate decoration on which the richness of their design depends. The second priority was to provide sound new copings for the fourteen traceried flying buttress arms, all badly decayed on top, and to replace the carved beasts which surmounted them. It also proved necessary to replace nearly all the upper parapets and pinnacles, if the Chapel was to regain its original silhouette.

It was decided that these structural elements were best replaced in hard-wearing Portland stone. Elsewhere, matching Bath stone was to be used to repair the body of the building. This would improve the effects of weathering by matching like with like and, just as important, it would avoid the visual disruption that results from the *ad hoc* patching with a lighter material that contrasts with the darker areas of original masonry. On a sophisticated structure like the Henry VII Chapel, such mixed repair would have been a visual disaster.

General repairs therefore, kept to a minimum by careful cleaning, washing and *in situ* 'plastic' repairs in lime mortar, are in Bath stone throughout. A few over-conspicuous sections of earlier repair in Portland have been removed. The contrast with the 'working' parts—parapets, pinnacles, buttress tops and cupolas—that have been robustly rebuilt in carefully selected Portland, which seems lighter than the Bath stone of the rest, strengthens rather than weakens the overall architectural effect.

As a final, well-tried method of conservation, all the new as well as the remaining Bath stone has, as in the 1820s, been once again heavily limewashed in an ochre colour. Perhaps if this treatment were to be repeated over a twenty year cycle, it might never be necessary to carry out major repairs again. As Lethaby advocated sixty years ago, such a course would be well worth trying!

Perhaps the outstanding aspect of the work carried out on the Henry VII Chapel has been the replacement of almost all the external ornament in a style based on medieval precedent and equal in vigour to the Gayfere restoration. Over three hundred major pieces of carving—including Tudor badges, lions, dragons and talbots—have been refashioned, besides the decorative work done on hundreds of crockets, finials and carved open parapet work. This has been a prodigious achieve-

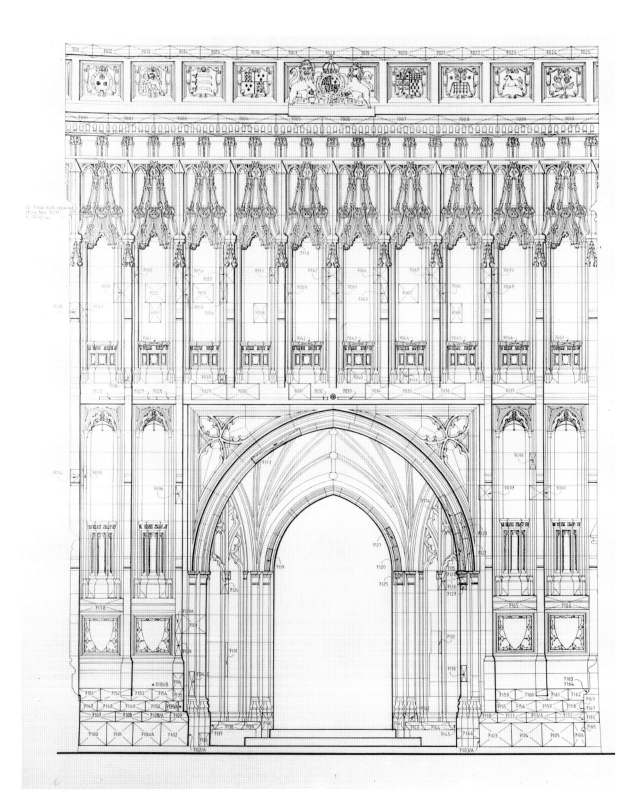

64. The Western Portal, drawn under the direction of the Surveyor in 1990 by Rattee & Kett

65. The Western Portal after repair, 1994

ment by six or seven carvers, working under the direction of Rattee and Kett's chief carver, Tim Crawley, for more than three years. It can be reckoned to be one of the most extensive programmes of architectural carving carried out this century. Within the limits set by the Surveyor and tested in models and trials, the carvers have been allowed much freedom. Over this period, their skills have developed in a way equal to anything done in the past.

Internally, minor repairs have been made to the upper and lower roof timbers, by improving gutters, falls and layout. The lead roof coverings have been recast and relaid and new and improved decorative lead rainwater heads have been provided. In September 1994, as external repairs neared completion, a further programme of internal work began, with complete scaffolding filling the Chapel for the first time since 1932. Special precautions were necessary to protect the outstanding contents of the Chapel while the vault and walls were cleaned, washed and limewashed. Particular attention was given to the exceptional medieval statuary (Cat. no. 13). These works will have been concluded in May 1995 with the installation of a new heraldic window placed at the west end. Devised by the Surveyor of the Fabric and designed by John Lawson of the Goddard & Gibbs studio, it commemorates the completion of the programme of restoration which has run from 1973 to 1995.

Detailed information on earlier restorations, even those of the nineteenth and early twentieth century, is far from complete, with drawings and other primary documents sadly often missing. This latest restoration, on the other hand, has created a great archive of record material, which will be made available to future generations. Several hundred drawings, thousands of photographs, detailed progress reports, and minutes of meetings have been preserved besides a great number of specialist historical and archaeological studies. This collection of material—like this exhibition—will be valuable in itself; but, just as important, these papers will provide an essential framework and reference for future works. All great buildings change if they are to remain alive: they live on only through the continued care of each succeeding generation.

Notes

Preface

1. Morris, 1900, pp. 44–45.
2. See Cat. no. 17.

I. The Medieval Abbey

1. Harvey, 1993, p. 2.
2. Harvey, 1977, p. 23.
3. Referred to as 'quire' in Westminster Abbey.
4. Barlow, 1992, p. 70.
5. Gem, 1980, p. 40. The plinths of the western piers, excavated in 1930, had been significantly altered; ibid., p. 44.
6. Tim Tatton-Brown, personal communication.
7. Harvey, 1977, pp. 28, 82–85.
8. Colvin, *King's Works*, Vol. 1, pp. 132 and 134.
9. ibid., Vol. 1, p. 494.
10. The sacristy built in Henry's time in the angle between the North Transept and the nave is poorly recorded and seems to have made little impact on the architecture of the main building.
11. Rackham, 1910, pp. 272–73.
12. Colvin, *King's Works*, Vol. 1, p. 135.
13. ibid., Vol. 1, p. 146.
14. ibid., Vol. 1, pp. 55–56; *New Bell's Cathedral Guides*, 1986, p. 30.
15. The outer porch added to the North Front in about 1360 may have been intended to shelter an image or chapel, rather than to improve access to the building.
16. *New Bell's Cathedral Guides*, 1986, p. 32.
17. For example Lethaby, 1906, p. 144.
18. Colvin, *King's Works*, Vol. 3, p. 215.

II. From Reformation to Refoundation

1. O'Neilly and Tanner, 1966, p. 124 note 2.
2. It has also been argued that the canopy dates from the last years before the Dissolution, O'Neilly and Tanner, 1966, pp. 150–53.
3. Hacket, 1692–93, Vol. 1, p. 45.
4. id., Vol. 1, pp. 211–12.

5. There is a note however in the accounts concerning the removal of the altar by a mason, Henry Wilson.
6. Quoted in Carpenter, 1966, p. 172.
7. Pepys, 1970, Vol. 1, p. 252.
8. WAM 44024.
9. cf. Chapter IV, p. 65.
10. *New Bell's Cathedral Guides*, 1986, p. 43.
11. Brayley, 1818–23, Vol. 2, p. 15; Lethaby, 1925, p. 67.
12. Colvin pointed out the apparent confusion in the Chapter books between Edward and Robert; Colvin, 1978, p. 913.
13. Hooke, 1935, pp. 246 and 253.
14. WAM 34592B.
15. WAM 34713 provides a resumé of the successive Acts of Parliament.

III. The Great Restoration

1. Christopher Wren's 'Memorial' printed in Wren, 1965, pp. 295–302 and Hawksmoor's letter of 1735 concerning his restoration of the Abbey is WAM 34576.
2. WAM 34521.
3. Brayley, 1818–23, Vol. 2, pp. 13 and 17.
4. WAM 34512 f.7.
5. McDowall et al., 1966, pp. 157–58. Unfortunately, the original roofs were recorded only in part before their removal in the 1960s.
6. WAM 34593.
7. WAM 34589.
8. Keepe, 1683, pp. 23–24.
9. Wren, 1965, p. 302.
10. Lincoln Chapter Archives, A/4/13, item 11.
11. Lethaby, 1925, p. 77.
12. Scott, 1863, p. 34.
13. The appearance of the portals between the removal of the porch, probably in the 1660s, and the Wren and Dickinson restoration is not recorded. The fact that they are shown the same in both the 'before' and 'after' views in the Dickinson drawing of 1719 (ill. 19) suggests that work at this level had already been

completed, possibly even before Wren's appointment in 1699.

14. However, Wyngaerde's drawing of Westminster of *c.* 1550 appears to show a pinnacle on the apex of the gable. Hence Wren may have had some archaeological authority for his reconstruction.

15. It is difficult to check Dickinson's design of the tracery shown by Hollar, since the depiction of the latter is imprecise. Several drawings by Dickinson survive showing variant designs for the tracery. Benton, 1983, *passim.*

16. Quoted in Colvin, 1978, p. 259.

17. Wren, 1965, pp. 300–301.

18. WAM (P) 907, 908, 909.

19. WAM (P) 908.

20. WAM (P) 907.

21. WAM 34660.

22. ibid., WAM 34661A, item 7.

23. ibid., WAM 34573.

24. A petition to Parliament as late as December 1743 referred to the possibility of a spire of the type shown in the Wren model; ibid., WAM 34720.

25. A petition to Parliament of about 1728 claimed that successive surveyors (Wren and Hawksmoor) had considered the rebuilding of the choir 'highly necessary' and this is supported by surviving drawings, for instance, WAM 34637.

26. WAM 34669 A.

27. The previous organ was on the north side of the choir just west of the crossing. Perkins, *Westminster Abbey,* Vol. 2, pp. 8–11.

28. Unpublished design in the Langley Collection in Westminster Abbey Library.

29. WAM 34517 f. 13; Neale and Brayley, 1818–23, Vol. 2, p. 38.

30. WAM 34662.

31. WAM 34698.

32. WAM 35002 A.

33. WAM 35111.

34. WAM 34875.

35. WAM 34915.

36. WAM 34660, 34549.

37. WAM 34512 f. 9.

38. WAM 34586. After the passing of the Fifty New Churches Act, the funds for Westminster Abbey were allocated as part of the grants under that Act.

39. WAM 34650.

40. WAM 34631 C.

41. WAM 34807: draft petition to Parliament of *c.* 1740.

42. WAM 34658 A: Draft Petition to Parliament of *c.* 1737.

43. WAM 39592: First petition to Parliament of 1696–7.

44. Quarrell and Mare, 1934, pp. 91–95.

45. Hunting, 1981, pp. 88–89.

46. See Cocke, 1979, pp. 71–77.

47. Cocke, 1985, p. 110.

48. Perkins, *Westminster Abbey*, Vol. 1, pp. 146–48.

49. Perkins' indignation at the use of wooden vaulting, rather than masonry, was ill-founded since wooden vaulting can be found in many medieval and seventeenth-century churches (e.g. York Minster and Winchester Cathedral). Perkins, *Westminster Abbey*, Vol. 1, p. 148.

50. Colvin, *King's Works*, Vol. 6, p. 516.

51. ibid., p. 516.

52. Browne, 1807, pp. 9–10.

53. WAM 66343 B, 52203–4.

54. WAM 66390.

55. Scott, 1879, p. 93.

56. WAM, RCO Box 6: Report by Pearson, June 1879.

57. Ayloffe, 1789, p. 4.

58. *Gentleman's Magazine,* 1843, Vol. 1, p. 152.

IV. The Victorian Era

1. See Summary of Building History.

2. Jordan, 1980, pp. 67–70.

3. Modern scholarship does not regard Scott's roof as an accurate reconstruction of the original, which was probably much lower in pitch. *New Bell's Cathedral Guides,* 1986, pp. 87–88. The iron structure within is entirely Victorian.

4. Report of 22 February 1854.

5. WAM, RCO Box 5: Letter of 3 April 1848.

6. WAM 66333–9.

7. WAM 66221.

8. WAM 66340.

9. WAM 66340: Blore's note of 4 July 1839.

10. WAM 66446.

11. Markland, 1843, pp. 64–65.

12. WAM 66446.

13. Surveyor's Reports WAM, RCO Box 5: 4 March 1878

14. A good summary of what was done in the mid nineteenth century is given in Poole, 1889, pp. 301–304.

15. Royal Commission, 1924, pp. 22–23.

16. WAM 66243 A.

17. Scott, 1879, p. 151.

18. ibid., p. 381.

19. Scott, 1863, p. 41.

20. WAM, RCO Box 5: Report of 15 March 1872.

21. *Ecclesiologist*, IX, 1849, p. 334.

22. Scott, 1879, p. 154.

23. WAM 66274.

24. WAM 66332.

25. WAM, RCO Box 5: Report of 2 June 1875.

26. See Cat. no. 41.

27. WAM, RCO Box 5: Letter of 24 February 1868.

28. WAM, RCO Box 5: Report of 4 March 1878.

29. WAM, RCO Box 5: Report of 16 July 1894.

30. See Lockett, 1993, p. 123.

31. WAM, RCO Box 5: Letter of 4 July 1876.

32. Jordan, 1980, p. 69.

33. WAM, RCO Box 5: Report of 6 February 1867)

34. WAM, RCO Box 6: Letter of 10 April 1879 from J O Scott to Dean Stanley.

35. Morris, 1900, pp. 40 and 44.

36. Lethaby, 1906, p. 63.

37. Prothero, 1893, Vol. 2, p. 283.

38. ibid., p. 279.

39. ibid., p. 281.

40. WAM, RCO Box 5: Letter from Scott to Thynne, 8 July 1867.

41. Carpenter, 1966, pp. 320–21.

42. WAM WAM, RCO Box 6: Letter of 10 December 1887.

43. WAM, RCO Box 5: Report of 22 February 1854.

44. WAM, RCO Box 5: Letter of 1 February 1864.

45. The fees for burials and fines for monuments went to the maintenance of the fabric, but those for admission to 'ornamental improvements' over and above the ordinary works of repair, Carpenter, 1966, p. 289.

46. Prothero, 1893, Vol. 2, pp. 306–307.

47. Morris complained in 1893 of 'the neglect of the most ordinary measures for keeping the Abbey clean and neat.' Morris, 1900, p. 36.

48. See p. 68 ff.

49. Carpenter, 1966, p. 288.

50. WAM, RCO Box 5.

51. WAM, RCO Box 5: Letter of 18 February 1871.

52. WAM, RCO Box 5: Letter of 15 February 1871.

53. WAM, RCO Box 6: Letter of 14 February 1888.

54. WAM, RCO Box 6: Report of June 1879. Unlike Scott, Pearson appears not to have noted the differing roles of Wren, Dickinson and Hawksmoor in the early eighteenth-century restoration of the Abbey.

55. WAM, RCO Box 6: Letter of 16 November 1896 to Canon Wilberforce. Pearson seems here to be less well informed than Wren of the extensive use of iron cramps sealed in with lead throughout the Middle Ages, for instance by the builders of the Salisbury spire. Cocke and Kidson, 1993, pp. 10–11.

56. WAM, RCO Box 5: Letter of February 1854.

57. ibid.

58. WAM, RCO Box 6: Letter 10 May 1893.

59. ibid.

60. Field, 1987, p. 56.

61. Perkins, *Westminster Abbey*, Vol. 1, pp. 166–67 note 2.

62. WAM, RCO Box 5: 12 February 1866.

63. WAM, RCO Box 5: Letter of 24 February 1868.

64. Perkins, 1960, p. 26.

65. ibid., pp. 41–42.

66. Carpenter, 1966, p. 310.

67. WAM 57664.

68. WAM 66301.

69. WAM, RCO Box 6: Letter of 19 March 1884.

70. WAM, RCO Box 5: Letter of 25 January 1873.

71. WAM 66344.

72. WAM 66350.

66. Romanesque capital with the Judgement of Solomon. Abbey Museum ▷

67-68. Fragments of scalloped Romanesque capitals [1]

Catalogue

1 a & b

Two Fragments of Romanesque Scalloped Capitals

c. 1150
Reigate Stone
a & b: 350 × 410 mm.
Dean and Chapter of Westminster

ills. 67, 68

These two fragments of capitals were found, according to tradition, with other Romanesque remains during the lowering of the choir floor by Blore in 1846–48, re-used as building rubble by later masons. There is no evidence of their original position within the Abbey, whether in the church or the precinct. They belonged to responds, rather than to the capitals of free-standing shafts. Their style is that of the mid twelfth century.

2 a & b

Two Capitals (perhaps from the Cloister)

c. 1120–30
(a) Oolitic Stone, 300 × 350 mm.
(b) Caen Stone, 200 × 300 mm.
Dean and Chapter of Westminster

ills. 69, 70

These capitals form part of a series found over the years in different locations around the Abbey precincts. They may have belonged originally to the arcade piers of the Romanesque cloister. The most famous capital in this series is the one depicting the Judgement of Solomon (now in the Abbey Museum, *ill. 66*), which features figures carved in high relief and of great dramatic force. The examples exhibited show how such carved features were cut about when re-used as masonry.

LITERATURE: Lethaby, 1925, pp. 33–35.

69-70. Romanesque capitals [2]

3

Fragment of Twisted Colonette from the Masonry Base of the Shrine of St Edward

1269 or later
Purbeck Stone (coloured inlay lost)
240 × 120 mm.
Dean and Chapter of Westminster

ill. 71

The dedication of a new shrine for the Confessor in 1269 formed the climax of Henry III's rebuilding of the Abbey. The masonry base was constructed either in time for that dedication or some ten years later, using the skills and style of the Cosmatesque masons who had laid the sanctuary floor. It has even been suggested that the Petrus Romanus who 'signed' the monument was the son of the Odericus who 'signed' the floor. In 1536, the Shrine was dismantled (probably including the masonry base), but was restored twenty years later by Abbot Feckenham. During this period, certain elements became detached and were only rediscovered by Scott in the mid nineteenth century, who successfully reintegrated a number of the pieces into the Shrine.

The exhibited fragment appears to have belonged to the north-east corner. It was discovered in 1904 outside the south end of Dean's Yard; so it was presumably one of the elements which was already missing when the Shrine was reconstructed. The original inlay of coloured tesserae has been lost on all but a few pieces.

LITERATURE: Scott, 1863, pp. 59–60; Perkins, *Westminster Abbey*, Vol. 2, pp. 76–77, 106–110; Binski, 1990, pp. 12–19.

71. Fragment of angle colonette from the Shrine of St Edward, held in position [3]

4 a & b

Fragments of Cable Moulding, probably associated with the Shrine of St Edward

c. 1269 or *c.* 1290
Purbeck Stone
a & b: 350 × 80 mm.
Dean and Chapter of Westminster

ill. 72

These fragments, like the terracotta pieces (Cat. no. 15), were apparently found in the blocking of the north window in the north west tower. Although similar in style to the material used for the Shrine (see Cat. no. 3) the fragments do not match any part of it. Perhaps they belonged to the image- or candle-stands which we know surrounded the Shrine. Lethaby associated a payment made in 1290 for three marble columns around the Shrine with these fragments.

LITERATURE: Poole, 1889, p. 116; Lethaby, 1925, p. 230.

72. Fragments of cable moulding [**4**]

73. Angel with harp [**5**]

5

Carved Angel with Harp from Spandrel of Wall Arcading

c. 1255–60
Probably Caen Stone
600 × 620 mm.
Dean and Chapter of Westminster

col. pl. V; ill. 73

Henry III's rebuilding of the Abbey was marked by a great richness of sculpted detail. The idea of placing carved angels in the spandrels of the wall arcading around the chapels and in those of the upper windows in the transepts derives from French models. A comparable scheme exists at the Sainte Chapelle in Paris, competition with which was evidently an important element in the design of Westminster. However, the motif is also found in the contemporary choir screen formerly in Salisbury Cathedral and in the Angel Choir at Lincoln Cathedral. According to Lethaby, the figure exhibited came from either the Chapel of St Nicholas or that of St Edmund.

LITERATURE: Lethaby, 1925, pp. 187–88.

6

Cast of Censing Angel in the Spandrel at the south-west corner of the South Transept

Original: *c.* 1255–60; Cast: 1931
Plaster
1400 × 1070 mm.
Dean and Chapter of Westminster

col. pl. VI

The figure is one of the most famous pieces of English sculpture surviving from the Middle Ages. The style, with its crisp folds and its use of a half-smile to animate the features, is related to sculpture at Rheims of the 1240s. This cast was taken in 1931 when scaffolding was erected for cleaning the interior of the South Transept. It was polychromed on the advice of Professor Tristram following surviving traces of pigment and gilding. Thus, it gives a reasonably authentic impression of the colour of Henry III's Westminster. The interaction of figurative sculpture with both architecture and decoration would have produced a total, all-embracing effect on the beholder, such as can be experienced today more easily in buildings of the German Baroque rather than in surviving Gothic monuments.

LITERATURE: Lethaby, 1925, pp. 184–88, 207–8; Tanner, 1948, pp. 15–16; Lindley, 1994, pp. 240–41.

74. The Westminster Retable

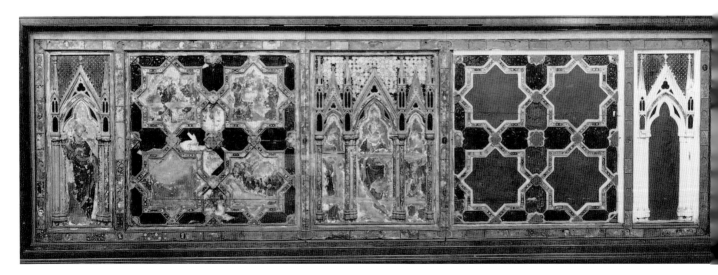

7

Copy of Figure of St Peter from the Westminster Retable

Original: *c.* 1270–90; Copy: 1827
Watercolour
705 × 330 mm.
Private Collection

ills. 74, 75

The Westminster Retable is one of the most precious survivals of the Court Style of painting during the reigns of Henry III and Edward I. Whether or not it acted as reredos to the High Altar is still disputed; but the exquisite quality of the painting and the recondite elements of its iconography demonstrate that it was an object of major value. The retable suffered an ignominious fate in post-medieval times by being re-used as part of a case for the collection of wooden and wax funerary effigies known as the Ragged Regiment. Noted by George Vertue in the mid eighteenth century, its significance was not fully recognized until Blore rescued it and had it suitably framed in 1827. The picture was then reproduced, not in one large engraving of the whole but in separate details, hence this watercolour drawing by J. Stephanoff. It now gives valuable evidence as to the condition of the figure at the time of the rediscovery of this all too fragile object.

LITERATURE: Lethaby, 1925, pp. 254, 274, (manuscript note by Tanner in grangerized copy in Westminster Abbey Library); Binski, 1995, pp. 153–67.

75. Copy of the figure of St Peter
from Westminster Retable [7]

115

8

Fragments of Grisaille Glass

c. 1250–1300
Stained glass
1650 × 1320 mm.
The Dean and Chapter of Westminster

col. pl. IV

These fragments of glass were amongst those gathered together by Henry Poole, Clerk of Works to Scott during the restorations of the Abbey in the 1860s and 1870s. They form a reminder of the rich array of stained glass which must have existed in the medieval Abbey. The surviving glass dates from several periods. Glass from the reign of Henry III was gathered during the Wren restoration by the glazier Edward Drew and set into the windows of the apse. Other fragments were placed in the windows of St Edmund's Chapel and under the West Towers. The most famous scenes, notably the Stoning of St Stephen, are the thirteenth-century panels preserved in the Abbey Museum. The fragments exhibited were apparently discovered in 1868, like those reinstated in 1908 in the west aisle of the North Transept, in a window in the east wall of the Chapel of St Nicholas, blocked by a buttress during the construction of the Henry VII Chapel. Grisaille was not a poor alternative to figurative scenes but was valued in its own right and as frame and background to figurative panels.

LITERATURE: *New Bell's Cathedral Guides*, 1986, pp. 111–12; Lethaby, 1925, pp. 234–35, 251; Poole, 1889, p. 187.

9

Polychrome Figure of Our Lady

c. 1300–25
Probably Reigate Stone
670 × 230 mm.
Dean and Chapter of Westminster

col. pl. III

It is not clear where this statue was first set up or where it was rediscovered in post-medieval times. By the early 1920s it was placed over the entrance to St Erasmus's Chapel (which presumably explains the crude inscription 'Saint Emrmus' [*sic*] on its rear face). In the 1970s it re-emerged in a former coal hole off the Dark Cloister.

The exhibited piece is a rare survivor of the images which once crowded the Abbey. Despite extensive damage to the features, the polychrome decoration is comparatively well preserved, unlike other sculpture in the Abbey. (I am grateful to Pamela Tudor-Craig for discussing this figure with me.) The battered state of the figure is also a vivid illustration of how figurative sculpture could be unsentimentally re-used as building material.

10

Decorated Tiles

c. 1250–1350
Earthenware
160 × 230 mm. (average size)
Dean and Chapter of Westminster

ill. 76

The floors of Westminster Abbey, though chiefly famous for the inlaid Cosmatesque pavements in the Sanctuary and around the Shrine, included some fine examples of tile work. The mid thirteenth-century tile floor in the Chapter House is particularly well preserved, ironically because of

76. Fragments of decorated tiles [**10**]

centuries of concealment under a wooden floor while the building was in secular use as a repository of records. The exhibited examples include motifs such as the fish, which are also found in the Chapter House. They can also be compared to the fourteenth-century tiles still *in situ* in the Chapel of St Faith, the Pyx Chapel and the Muniment Room.

117

11

Fragments from a Heraldic Panel

c. 1450–1500
Caen Stone
1300 × 430 mm.
Dean and Chapter of Westminster

ill. 77

These fragments were found, together with several similar pieces, when the pinnacles of the flying buttresses along the south side rebuilt by Scott were again reconstructed by Foster in 1984. Presumably, they had originally been recycled as building materials when the buttresses had been rebuilt during the Wren and Hawksmoor restorations and had then escaped recognition by the nineteenth-century masons. Despite ill usage, traces of colour still remain. Their original setting is unknown; although they are likely to have formed part of a tomb or screen. On stylistic grounds, they can be dated to *c.* 1450–1500. Well before the Dissolution, the Abbey was being filled with heraldic decoration relating to tombs or major donors.

12

Elements from Tomb Railings

c. 1440
Wrought iron
2650 × 120 mm.
Dean and Chapter of Westminster

cf. ill. 78

The railings exhibited are impressive examples of late medieval wrought iron work, probably designed to enclose the east side of the tomb chest of Henry V. Any substantial monument was surrounded by protective railings, whether in the Middle Ages or in the seventeenth or eighteenth century. The pilfering and petty damage suffered by many Abbey monuments show that this was a wise precaution. It was only in the early nineteenth century that railings began to be taken away, partly on aesthetic grounds and also because public manners were deemed to have improved to a degree that monuments would be better respected. In the Abbey, most railings were removed, apparently on the advice of Sir Francis Chantrey, as part of the rearrangements consequent upon the Coronation of George IV. The railings belonging to the tomb of Queen Eleanor (died 1290) were reinstated by Scott in 1849.

LITERATURE: Lethaby, 1925, p. 290.

77. Fragments of a heraldic panel [11]

78. Engraving, *c.* 1800, showing former railings to the tomb of Henry V [12]

13 a & b

Two Statues from the Henry VII Chapel: (a) St Katherine, (b) St Matthew

c. 1510
(a) Reigate Stone
(b) Caen Stone
a & b: 1080 × 370 mm.
Dean and Chapter of Westminster

col. pls. VII, VIII

The Henry VII Chapel was not only a building of exceptional architectural elaboration, it was also decorated 'in as goodly and as riche maner as suche a werk requireth, and as to a King's werk apperteigneth.' (Colvin, *King's Works*, Vol. 3, p. 215). There were originally one hundred and seven stone images, of which ninety-five remain: the most complete set of its kind to survive in England. It was intended that they should be 'painted garnished and adorned'; but there is little evidence of how this decoration was carried out. Some traces of under-painting have been detected. The images on the exterior of the building represented the Apostles, the Patriarchs and the Kings of Judah. The images inside included a spectacular array of saints, 'all the holie companie of Heaven', according to King Henry's will. In the early eighteenth century, those figures remaining on the outside were removed for safety and stored above the chapel vaults. It is possible, however, that some images have since been placed within the Chapel since several statues, such as the figure of St Katherine, show signs of weathering.

LITERATURE: Colvin, *King's Works*, Vol. 3, pp. 215–17.

14 a & b

Two Sections of Traceried Panelling from the Henry VII Chapel

c. 1505–9
(a) Oolitic Stone, 440 × 750 mm.
(b) Caen Stone, 440 × 560 mm.
Dean and Chapter of Westminster

ills. 79, 80

These are two examples of carved medieval stonework which survived the refacing of the exterior of the Henry VII Chapel between 1809 and 1822. According to Thomas Gayfere, the conscientious mason who superintended the operation, the Chapel was originally constructed from a variety of stones: Kentish Ragstone in the foundations; 'Kentish stone'—finer in grain than the rag—in the plinth; Huddlestone from Yorkshire in the flying buttresses; Caen stone in the superstructure and Reigate stone from Surrey for internal screens. The smaller block **(b)** is re-used material. It may have come from Queen Elizabeth Woodville's Chapel of St Erasmus demolished after only a few decades to make place for the Henry VII Chapel. Traces of Perpendicular detailing can been seen on the former face of the block, which was reversed when it was re-used by the early nineteenth-century masons.

LITERATURE: Neale and Brayley (1818), Vol. II, appendix, pp. 51–52.

79-80. Sections of tracery panels from the Henry VII Chapel [**14**]

a

b

15 a, b & c

Fragments of Terracotta Figures, perhaps associated with the workshops of Pietro Torrigiano or Benedetto da Rovezzano

c. 1510–30
Terracotta
(a) foot and drapery: 440 × 750 mm.
(b) arm and drapery: 800 × 600 mm.
(c) lower part of fringed robe: 320 × 260 mm.
Dean and Chapter of Westminster

ills. 81-83

These pieces are three of a number of terracotta fragments discovered in 1868 blocking window openings in the north west tower. They may have been discarded after problems in their manufacture and were re-used as rubble fill. Alternatively, they may have been victims of iconoclasm. They belong to a small series of terracotta sculptures made in the first quarter of the sixteenth century in England. The series has been associated with either Pietro Torrigiano (1472–1528), the Florentine responsible for the effigies of Henry VII, his wife Elizabeth of York and his mother Margaret Beaufort, or with Benedetto da Rovezzano (1474–*c.*1552), another Florentine who worked in England for at least ten years on Cardinal Wolsey's tomb. Although broken into many small pieces, these fragments display a quality of modelling worthy of such artists.

LITERATURE: Gunn and Lindley, 1991, pp. 270, 279.

a

b

c

81-83. Fragments of terracotta figures [15]

121

16

Charter of Philip and Mary refounding the Monastic Community at Westminster

1556
Parchment
Section exhibited: 850 × 950 mm.
Dean and Chapter of Westminster

col. pl. XI

The accession of Mary I in 1553, and her re-establishment of traditional Catholic practices and of England's allegiance to the Papacy, did not at first extend to the revival of the monasteries dissolved by her father twenty years before. Westminster remained a co-cathedral of the Diocese of London, served by a Dean and Chapter. However, by 1555, Mary was encouraging a group of Benedictine monks, led by John Feckenham, to return to the Abbey. The then Dean, Hugh Weston, Marian partisan though he was, prevaricated and it was not until the autumn of 1556 that the Chapter was dissolved and the monks reinstated. The revived monastery did not last long, being dissolved in July 1559. But the refoundation by Philip and Mary had a permanent effect on the Abbey's future. It ended Westminster's role as a cathedral and re-established it as a unique entity, created by a deliberate act of royal favour. This status survived the doctrinal changes of Elizabeth giving the church its special role in national life.

This charter, issued on 10 November 1556, is prefaced with miniature portraits of Philip and Mary, according to tradition. Despite their unsophisticated style, the miniatures present memorable images of the joint sovereigns. Few people remember that Philip II of Spain, who sent the Armada against England, had been King of England for four years and had worshipped in state at Westminster.

LITERATURE: Knowles, 1979, pp. 424–34.

17

Effigy of Elizabeth I

1603 and 1760
Wax work (for the head) and wooden armature (for the body)
1750 × 1100 mm.
Dean and Chapter of Westminster

col. pls. IX, X; ills. 84, 85

Queen Elizabeth holds a special place in the history of Westminster Abbey, echoing that of the Confessor. The refoundation of 1560 owed something to her father's charters of 1540 and 1542 in its strong emphasis on Westminster School and the links with the universities and to her sister's charter of 1556 in its recognition of the individual nature of the Abbey under its royal patron.

After the death of Elizabeth, her cult flourished in the Abbey and throughout the nation. Her Accession Day of 17 November was celebrated with bonfires until well into the 18th century and her tomb in the Abbey was copied in many churches as a kind of memorial. Thus, it was no accident that the decayed funerary effigy of Elizabeth was refashioned at the time of the bicentenary of the Refoundation in 1760 with a replica head and new robes of high quality. The sensitive modelling of the features was presumably taken from the tomb effigy by Maximilian Colt (or from the original head which was being replaced). The rich apparel of the effigy's robes and jewellery is important evidence of the romantic antiquarianism of the 1750s and its appreciation of 'King James' Gothic' (as the mixed 'Jacobethan' style was called), rather than a faithful following of the original. The recently completed conservation has revealed that, contrary to the previous assessment of the effigy as an entirely 18th-century creation, the original armature survives, together with two under-garments, 'a paire of straight bodies' (or stays) and 'a paire of drawers,' which are some of the earliest known examples of their kind. This exhibition provides the first opportunity to see all the elements of the effigy.

LITERATURE: Harvey and Mortimer, 1994, pp. 126–30.

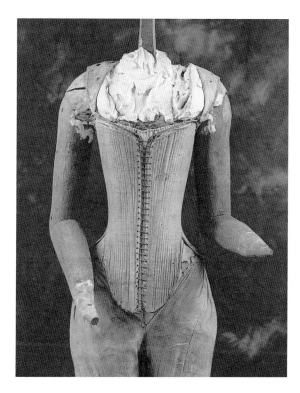

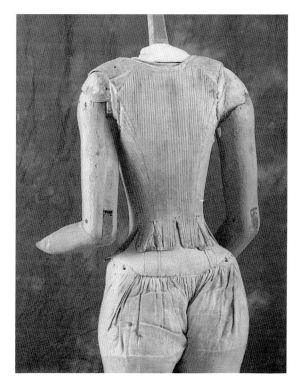

18

Cope made for the Coronation of Charles II

1660–1
Purple velvet
1600 × 1200 mm.
Dean and Chapter of Westminster

col. pls. XVI, XVII

The Coronation of Charles II on St George's Day 1661 was celebrated with particular care and solemnity to mark the restoration of both Monarchy and Church. After the depredations of the Interregnum, it was necessary to replace both the regalia and the vestments for the officiating clergy, presumably dispersed in 1643. Copes of both purple and crimson velvet were made, presumably those recorded in the archives as costing, together with other unspecified vestments, the considerable sum of £1,031. They are powdered with pomegranates (on the purple set) or five-petalled flowers (on the crimson), trefoils, and stars worked in gold and silver thread. These vestments have survived wear and tear, neglect (especially in the late 18th and 19th centuries) and periodic restoration. Their existence is striking testimony to the care of the re-established Church of England to preserve the 'beauty of holiness' and the traditional ways overturned by the Civil War.

LITERATURE: Perkins, *Westminster Abbey*, Vol. 3 pp. 74–83.

84–85. Front and back view of the undergarments from the original effigy of Queen Elizabeth I

86. Helmet from Hatton Monument [19]

87. The Hatton Monument, present state

19

Helmet from the Monument to Sir Christopher Hatton and his Wife, Alise Fanshaw

c. 1620
Alabaster
330 × 240 mm.
Dean and Chapter of Westminster

ills. 86, 87

The monument to Sir Christopher Hatton (died 1619) and his wife, Alise Fanshaw (died 1623), was originally placed against the east wall of the Islip Chapel. It was moved to the triforium of the North Transept in 1940, when an altar was reinstated in the Chapel. The design, as reassembled, now appears uncoordinated, but it was well suited in a 'singular taste' to its original site.

The permission granted to a Jacobean courtier not only for burial but also for the erection of a large monument in the Abbey marks how widely those privileges had become shared among the nobility and gentry by the early seventeenth century. Despite the classical style of such monuments, they did not abandon the heraldic display of the late Middle Ages, including helmets such as this one. The carving clearly depicts a close-helmet of the period, perhaps made in a Greenwich workshop for use in tournaments. The gauntlet on which it rested has unfortunately been lost.

The partial dismantling of monuments or, in some cases, their banishment to the triforium have been fates meted out to a good number of post-medieval tombs from the mid nineteenth century to the present day. The reasons for such action was either to reveal more of the Gothic structure of the Abbey or, as here, to restore a chapel to liturgical use.

LITERATURE: Royal Commission, 1924, p. 75; Ackermann and Combe, 1812, Vol. 1, p. 183.

20 a & b

Two Kneeling Angels from former 'Whitehall' Altarpiece, by Grinling Gibbons and Arnold Quellin

1686
Marble
(a) 1350 × 940 mm.
(b) 1250 × 860 mm.
Vicar and Churchwardens
of St Andrew's, Burnham-on-Sea

ills. 88, 89

In 1706 Queen Anne gave to the Abbey the altarpiece which had been constructed thirty years earlier for the Roman Catholic chapel built for her father, James II, by Sir Christopher Wren in Whitehall Palace, but which had lain in store in Hampton Court following the Glorious Revolution. It was a work of exceptional quality, designed by Wren and adorned with sculptures by Grinling Gibbons (1648–1721) and Arnold Quellin (1653–86). It is not clear how much adaptation was necessary to fit it into Westminster, which, in architectural style, proportions and iconography could hardly have been a more different setting from the original. Wren and Gibbons were still alive and were, no doubt, careful to ensure that the alterations were sensitively done. The altarpiece rose in three stages. The altar was recessed between side panels, adorned by cherubs; above, the central feature was a large gilded panel inscribed with the Gloria. This was in turn surmounted by a symbol of the Holy Name, encircled by cherub heads and flanked by the two angels here exhibited. Although so different from the Gothic monuments around the apse, the scale of the altarpiece and its fine materials must have recaptured the vertical focus at the heart of the Abbey, lost by the destruction of both the tall rood and the Confessor's reliquary during the Reformation.

The altarpiece was removed to increase the seating accommodation at the Coronation of George IV and was then discarded. A few pieces remained at Westminster, including the life-size statues now sadly weather-worn in the College garden and two reliefs eventually housed in the

125

88-89. Angels from the former 'Whitehall' Altarpiece [20]

Museum. But the majority of pieces went to the parish of Burnham-on-Sea in Somerset, a living held by Walker King, the then Bishop of Rochester and formerly prebend at the Abbey. The relief panels of putti and the inscribed Gloria were reassembled there as a reredos, flanked by the two adoring angels and topped by the Sacred Name. When this arrangement was in turn dismantled in the late nineteenth century, four reliefs were used in a new reredos and the remainder housed in the west tower.

The angels differ in style. Angel (a) is carved in a more robust and Baroque manner, although with the features broadly treated. Angel (b) is calmer and the face has larger and more strongly characterized features. The former might be attributed to Quellin and the latter to Gibbons. As set up in the Abbey, angel (b) was on the north side and angel (a) on the south side. It is probable that the poses of both the arms and wings have been altered in the successive locations.

LITERATURE: Colvin, *King's Works*, Vol. 5, pp. 285–93; Perkins, *Westminster Abbey*, Vol. 1, pp. 65–80; Wren Society, 1930, pp. 74–75, 81–86, 236–39; Green, 1962, pp. 164–66; Vivian-Neal, 1935, pp. 127–32.

21

**Head of a Cherub
(probably from former Organ Case)**

c. 1728
Oak
240 × 340 mm.
Dean and Chapter of Westminster

ill. 90

The date and provenance of this fine cherub's head are not established for certain, but it probably belonged on the west face of the organ case given by George II in 1728. Although such furnishings, like the great Queen Anne reredos (see Cat. no. 20), have vanished, they were evidently of high quality.

90. Head of a Cherub from former organ case [**21**]

127

22

Pair of Pyramids
once flanking the Choir Entry

c. 1680–1700
Oak
2750 × 460 mm.
Dean and Chapter of Westminster

ills. 91, 92

These 'pyramids' once formed the crowning finials of the giant gate piers built to flank the entry through the choir screen in the late seventeenth century. No evidence has yet been found of the medieval treatment of the west face of the screen or the reasons which made its reconstruction necessary. Perhaps the prominent imagery which must have been associated with it before the Reformation had led to more determined iconoclasm in this part of the church and thus to more damage to the screen. The late seventeenth-century scheme was most unusual: monumental square piers, apparently articulated with Doric pilasters, carried these tall tapering spires, clearly designed to evoke Gothic pinnacles. No documentary evidence has been identified to establish either a date or its designer. It would be tempting to link such an imaginative reconciliation of the antique and the medieval with Hawksmoor; but the only depiction of the composition *in situ* dates from *c.* 1715, before he was involved in the Abbey (see print by J. Cole in Dart, 1723, Vol. 1, opposite p. 68). It was Hawksmoor, in fact, who refashioned the screen in 1728 in a more conventional manner with a central archway, so that it could carry the new organ (see Cat. no. 21).

The carving of the two cherub heads that survive is extremely fine, perhaps executed by the same craftsmen who produced the 'Whitehall' altarpiece (see Cat. no. 20). Alas, the storage of these exceptional features in the south west tower and mistreatment subsequent to their rediscovery in 1862 have damaged them greatly.

LITERATURE: Perkins, *Westminster Abbey*, Vol. 2, pp. 8–11.

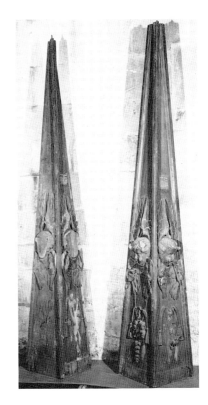

91. Pyramids from the former Choir Screen [22]

92. Decorative detail on one of the pyramids [22]

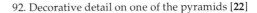

93. Engraving showing the Choir Screen with pyramids, *c.* 1710

94. Section of inscribed lead roofing [23]

23 a & b

Sections of Lead Roofing

1779 and 1821
Lead
(a) 490 × 260 mm.
(b) 450 × 300 mm.
Dean and Chapter of Westminster

ill. 94

These sections of worn-out lead roofing, preserved for the sake of their inscriptions, are reminders of the ceaseless work—rarely recorded—necessary to keep the Abbey roofs in good repair. The date 1779 does not correspond to any major restoration campaign, coming some decades after Dean Wilcocks had renewed all the lead roofing, as is recorded in his epitaph. The lead roof of 1821 might perhaps be connected with the restoration of the Henry VII Chapel. While the lead covering must have been recast many times, the original medieval timber roofs survived the Dissolution, wars and restoration, only to be removed in large part during the 1960s.

LITERATURE: McDowell et al., passim.

24

Christopher Wren's Model for a proposed Central Spire

c. 1720
Oak and pear wood
2360 × 950 mm.
Dean and Chapter of Westminster

ill. 95

The work on the Abbey subsidised by the Parliamentary grant of 1697 specifically included both 'repairing' and 'finishing.' In this latter category came the West Towers (still left at the level reached by the 1530s) and the unimpressive lantern over the crossing. Henry III had not completed this part of his plan and at the coronation of his successor the crossing was simply boarded over internally. (Colvin, *King's Works*, Vol. 1, p. 146 note 7). There is no evidence that a more substantial solution was attempted over the succeeding four centuries, or that a tower or *flèche* was ever erected. Wren recorded in his 'Memorial' of 1713 that 'the original intention was plainly to have had a steeple' both for aesthetic reasons and to stabilize the structure. Addressing his own day, he added that the spire would give 'a proper grace to the whole fabric' and to the surrounding townscape (Wren, 1965, p. 301). He planned to strengthen the crossing piers in order to support the added weight (see Cat. no. 25b)

It is not clear which of the many variant designs for a central spire became the preferred solution of Wren or his associates, Dickinson and Hawksmoor. The model demonstrates a conventional late medieval arrangement with a tall 'belfry' stage topped by a twelve-sided spire. Other drawings and prints show experiments with polygonal drums and domes, resembling Wren's early designs for the central steeple at St Paul's and his Tom Tower at Christ Church, Oxford. This model was probably constructed before 1724 when a low lantern was erected. Hawksmoor was still hoping for some form of crowning cupola at the time of his death in 1736. The model collapsed following water damage during the Second World War but was carefully repaired by J. G. O'Neilly for exhibition in 1981.

LITERATURE: Hunting, 1981, pp. 36–38, 210; Wren, 1965, pp. 300–301.

95. Christopher Wren's model for a central spire [24]

The North Front of y.ᵉ Collegiate Church of Westminster
With y.ᵉ 2 West Towers and the middle Lantren as intended.

25 a, b, c

Three Designs for the Abbey
by Nicholas Hawksmoor

(a) The North Front 'with ye two West Towers and the middle lantern as intended,'
(b) Plan of crossing, choir and nave with 'the legs of ye middle tower made thicker'
(c) Proposed spires on the West Towers
1724–1735
Pen and wash
(a) 510 × 690 mm.
(b) 490 × 905 mm.
(c) 770 × 540 mm.
Dean and Chapter of Westminster

ills. 96, 97, 98

Nicholas Hawksmoor succeeded Wren as Surveyor of the Abbey on the latter's death in 1723. William Dickinson, who had acted as Under-Surveyor and virtual deputy to Wren in his later years, died eighteen months later. Thus, Hawksmoor had the opportunity not only to continue, but to recast significant elements within the restoration programme. Like Wren and Dickinson, he was anxious to enliven the skyline of the Abbey with steeples at the crossing and at the West End. Hawksmoor did achieve the completion of the western towers and the erection of a low lantern at the crossing; but the various cupolas and spires which he proposed never left the drawing board.

While several Hawksmoor drawings for the Abbey have been known for years, a volume containing further designs, together with other loose drawings, was recently acquired by the Dean and Chapter of Westminster thanks to generous grants by the National Art-Collections Fund, the National Heritage Memorial Fund and the Manifold Trust. Subsequent conservation work has allowed certain flaps to be lifted, revealing alternative versions—more evidence of the fertility of Hawksmoor's imagination.

LITERATURE: Worsley, 1993, pp. 100–101.

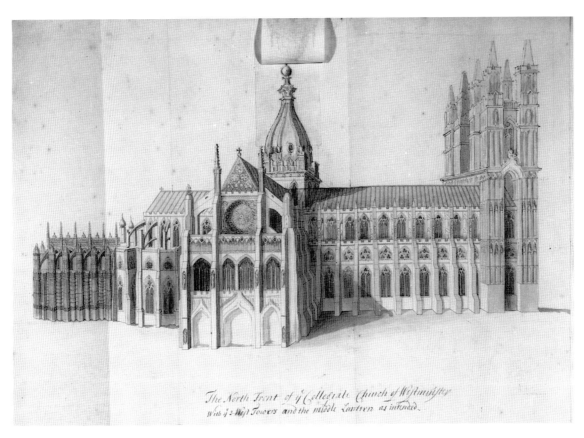

The North Front of y͠e Collegiate Church of Westminster
With y͠e 2 West Towers and the middle Lantren as intended.

The North Front of y͠e Collegiate Church of Westminster
With y͠e 2 West Towers and the middle Lantren as intended.

96–98. Three proposals by Nicholas Hawksmoor for a central steeple
and West Towers, as revealed by a series of flaps [25a]

99. Westminster Abbey with proposed steeples and dome. Painting by Pietro Fabris [26]

26

View of Abbey, from the north
by Pietro Fabris

c. 1735–40
Oil on canvas
840 × 1300
Dean and Chapter of Westminster

ill. 99

Until street widening and house clearances were carried out to the east and west of the Abbey, the north side was that most open to public view. However, this side was also blocked, by both the church and churchyard of St Margaret's and by the houses built up against the nave from the fourteenth century onwards, the removal of which was one of the conditions of the Parliamentary grants to the Wren restoration. The houses by the nave were demolished in 1740 but others to the east survived until the turn of the

century and even later. They were useful to the Chapter partly for the sake of their rents but partly because Westminster School occupied many of the former monastic buildings, leaving relatively little accommodation for the canons and the Abbey staff. The painting is by Pietro Fabris (*c.* 1735–1772), an Italian of Neapolitan background working in London in the mid eighteenth century. The work was presumably executed *c.* 1735, when the intention to erect a central steeple and to heighten the West Towers was known but no official design had been published and construction had yet to begin. It is not clear whether the artist's particular design for the centre spire shown in the painting had any authority from architect or Chapter. The painting was bought in Rome in 1826 and eventually presented to the Dean and Chapter by Lord Wakefield of Hythe in 1932.

LITERATURE: Tanner, 1969, p. 173.

27

View of the Choir, from the west, by an anonymous artist

c. 1700
1530 × 1290 mm.
Oil on canvas
Dean and Chapter of Westminster

ill. 100

This view, taken from on top of the screen, shows the interior of the choir as it must have appeared during the early years of the Wren restoration, before the introduction of the 'Whitehall' altarpiece in 1706. Depicted in the foreground are the thirteenth-century stalls and canopies (destroyed in the 1770s) and the lozenge-pattern floor laid at the expense of Doctor Busby, a famous Headmaster of Westminster School and Prebendary of the Abbey in 1687. Past the crossing, with the organ tucked away to the north and the pews erected by Dean Neile 'for the better sort to sit in,' we see the altar, richly hung with 'purple velvet and satin wrought about and flowered with gold.' The picture was given to the Dean and Chapter in 1931 by the Reverend Pomfret Waddington, but nothing is known of its history.

LITERATURE: Perkins, *Westminster Abbey*, Vol. 1, pp. 62–64, 126, 128–30.

100. Interior of the Choir, *c.* 1700 [**27**]

101. St Luke from a study for stained glass, by Sir James Thornhill [**28a**]

28 a & b

Two Studies for Stained Glass in the North Transept Rose Window by Sir James Thornhill

(**a**) St Luke
(**b**) St John the Evangelist
c. 1720
a & b: 1000 × 2190 mm.
Oil on canvas
Rector and Churchwardens
of St Andrew's, Chinnor

col. pl. XV; ill. 101

In the early 1720s, the North Transept was extensively restored. Its external architecture was reconstructed in a sympathetic Gothic by William Dickinson and the great rose window was cleared of the plaster blocking some of its lights and reglazed with an ambitious programme of stained glass. The programme, the figure of Christ surrounded by the Apostles and Evangelists, was designed by Sir James Thornhill (1675–1734), then at the height of his fame, and executed by Joshua Price. These full-size cartoons were presumably painted for the glazier, since the outline of the cusped tracery lights is drawn out.

Luckily, the full set of studies, sold at auction after Thornhill's death, had been installed in Chinnor Church by 1759, possibly owing to family connections between the Thornhills and the owner of the Chinnor advowson. Even more luckily, the canvases survived the Victorian restoration of the church and are still hung there, where they have undergone recent conservation. (My thanks are due to Miss J. Cray who has both researched the history of the paintings and promoted their restoration). The stained glass itself was less fortunate. The redesigning of the rose by Pearson in the 1880s meant that the principal lights were reduced in size and the figures had to be cropped at the feet in order to fit.

LITERATURE: Cray, 1990, pp. 789–93.

29

Fragments of Choir Furnishings designed by Henry Keene

1775
Oak
Door: 880 × 860 mm.
Dean and Chapter of Westminster

ill. 103

The replacement of the thirteenth-century choir stalls in 1775 by new furnishings designed by the then Surveyor, Henry Keene, has remained controversial. The practical reason behind the alteration was to obtain furnishings that could be moved at coronations and thus avoid the confusion experienced at that of George III in 1761. Some members of the Chapter wanted to remove the choir altogether from its traditional—but awkward—position athwart the crossing so that it could occupy the whole eastern arm, including the feretory. When such a scheme was considered in 1773, the Chapter requested designs from Keene, the young James Wyatt, later Surveyor

himself, and James Essex, who had recently been responsible for a similar removal of the choir at Ely Cathedral. After vigorous debate, the idea of moving the choir was abandoned. Keene was commissioned to construct on the traditional site a new set of stalls and screens in Flemish oak, with pinnacles of cast iron (the latter a common feature of the best Gothic Revival furnishings of the period but anathema after Pugin). Although a distinguished architect of the mid Georgian Gothic Revival, Keene's designs were not outstanding, perhaps on account of his failing health. The best feature, the palm tree pulpit, survives at Trottiscliffe Church, Kent, whither it had been banished in 1824. Save for these panels which could have come from either the stall fronts or from the screens across the transept and were worked up into a bookcase, the remaining woodwork was destroyed when the Blore furnishings were installed in the mid nineteenth century (see Cat. no. 42).

LITERATURE: Perkins, *Westminster Abbey*, Vol. 1, pp. 84–85, 133–48; ibid., Vol. III, pp. 36–38.

102. Detail of Henry Keene's crossing screen, *c.* 1775

103. Bookcase made from Henry Keene's furnishings [**29**]

30

Modello for Monument to John, Second Duke of Argyll, by Louis-François Roubiliac

1745
Terracotta
860 × 500 mm.
Trustees of the Victoria and Albert Museum
(no. 21-1888)

ill. 105

The installation of so many large monuments in the Abbey during the eighteenth century has been treated for the past century as an essentially negative development. At the time, however, they were regarded differently. At a practical level, the fees charged by the Dean and Chapter for their erection, which varied according to the size of the monument and the rank of the person involved, formed a significant element in the funds available for the building's maintenance. The tombs were also exemplars of the achievements of the nation and its great men, which were lifting Great Britain to unprecedented power. The competition between such memorials and the Gothic architecture of the Abbey—or even between each other—did not worry the viewer of the period either in England or abroad.

The second Duke of Argyll (1680–1743) was a Whig hero, famed for his eloquence—hence the prominence of the allegorical figure of Eloquence at the Duke's feet—who helped ensure that Scotland resisted Jacobite plotting and remained faithful to the Union of 1707. The tomb made to him in the South Transept by Louis-François Roubiliac (1705?–1762), finally erected four years after the modello was made, is one of the most successful of its period. Pevsner considered that 'in spirited portraiture and delicacy of draperies,' it 'is supreme and need...not fear comparison with any contemporary monument in France or Italy.'

LITERATURE: Pevsner, 1973, pp. 445–46; Baker, 1992, pp. 785–97.

104. Monument to the Second Duke of Argyll, present state

105. Modello for the monument to the Second Duke of Argyll by Louis-François Roubiliac [30]

31

Re-used Memorial Tablet

c. 1700
Marble
800 × 600 mm.
Dean and Chapter of Westminster

ill. 106

This tablet was recently discovered with the frame fully carved but with its painted inscription erased. During the eighteenth and early nineteenth centuries, a great variety of people sought burial within the precincts of the Abbey, either in the church itself or in the cloister. There was one fee for an interment, and another for a memorial.

Although it is impossible to attribute the workshop in which this tablet was made, the sophistication of its carving shows the quality of more modest memorials such as this one, a subject still to be explored. The exhibited tablet also demonstrates that grandees were not the only ones buried at Westminster. Many of less exalted rank could also find burial in the Abbey, especially in the cloisters.

32

View of South West Tower and South Side of Nave from outside the Jerusalem Chamber by John Coney

1806
Watercolour
460 × 300 mm.
Private Collection

ill. 107

This signed and dated watercolour by John Coney (1786–1833) showing the view of the south side of the Abbey is relatively unusual. Most artists chose to depict the more easily accessible north side. This watercolour shows the fabric some sixty years after the completion of the Wren and Hawksmoor restorations. Clearly depicted are the buttresses and pinnacles and the window mouldings in the simplified forms considered acceptable in the early eighteenth century. Also visible is the blocking of some windows in the upper levels, perhaps for monuments. In the nineteenth century, Scott rebuilt the buttresses and pinnacles and Pearson replaced the facing. Thus, few of the stones depicted are still to be seen today, except on the south west tower. The present crenellated parapet is a postwar reminiscence of the one depicted here, but it replaces a nineteenth-century parapet by Blore of a different openwork design.

106. Marble cartouche [31]

107. The south west tower from the Jerusalem Chamber, by John Coney [32]

108. View across the choir from the organ gallery by William Capon [**33**]

33

Interior of the Choir looking east from the Organ Gallery
by William Capon

c. 1780–1800
Pen and ink
810 × 595 mm.
Private Collection

ill. 108

This unusual view across the choir by William Capon (1757–1827) gives a vivid impression of how the stalls designed by Keene appeared in relation to the 'Whitehall' altarpiece given by Queen Anne. Although the styles of each element differed, their proportions seem to have been well matched. Perhaps the rather schematic lines of Keene's Gothic panelling mediated more effectively between the classicism of Wren's altarpiece and the Early English of Henry III's architecture than a more severely archaeological design would have done.

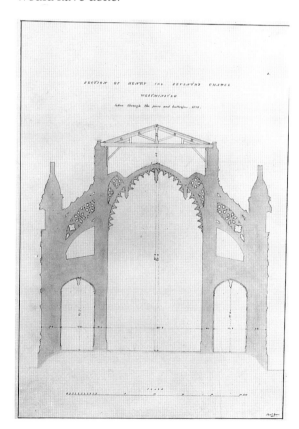

109. Section through the Henry VII Chapel by Samuel Ware [34]

34

Section through the Henry VII Chapel
by Samuel Ware

1810
Pen and ink with wash
445 × 315 mm.
Private Collection

ill. 109

The restoration of the Henry VII Chapel, financed by a Parliamentary grant in 1809–22, was both stimulated by and itself gave stimulus to the Gothic Revival. Although James Wyatt, the Surveyor of the Abbey, was savagely criticized by some contemporaries as the 'Great Destroyer' of medieval buildings, the works of restoration were conducted with great respect towards the medieval fabric. The mason responsible was Thomas Gayfere, whose father had also been mason to the Abbey and, incidentally, had assisted Horace Walpole at Strawberry Hill. Great care was taken in choosing the most suitable stone with which to reface the building and also in making casts of the surviving detailing.

Plans by the Dean and Chapter to restore the Chapel had been frustrated by the need to pay for extensive repairs after a destructive fire in 1803 which had also wrecked the lantern. Their new application to Parliament for public funds, made just a century after the original Parliamentary grant, proved successful and permitted a painstaking restoration, conducted from 1809 to 1822.

The famous pendant fan vault of the Chapel is one of the most daring constructions of the late medieval period. After a period of discredit in the late 17th century, when John Evelyn unfavourably compared its 'sharp angles, jetties, narrow lights, lame statues, lace and other cut-work and crinkle-crankle' with the clean, classical lines of Inigo Jones' Banqueting House or Christopher Wren's St Paul's, it was again admired in the 18th century (Evelyn, 1733, p. 9). This study was drawn by Samuel Ware (1781–1860), better known as architect of the Burlington Arcade, who had a particular interest in the structural properties of vaults.

LITERATURE: Ware, 1814, pp. 40–84; id., 1817, pp. 336–7.

35

View of the Henry VII Chapel
from the south-east, by Thomas Malton Jr.

c. 1796
Pencil, watercolour and body colour
840 × 1900 mm.
Collection of Donald Buttress

col. pl. XIV

The Henry VII Chapel, although it had been in-cluded in preliminary estimates, was not in the event worked on during the Wren and Hawk-smoor restorations. Thus, by the close of the eighteenth century, the exterior was badly de-cayed. The intricate display of sculpture and the 'crinkle-crankle' of the walling were vulnerable to passing damage from traffic and to corrosion by the coal smoke of London.

The picture by Thomas Malton Jr.(1748–1804) shows the disappearance of the crowning para-pet and pinnacles, which had to be replaced by Wyatt following a design unlikely to reflect the original. Also vanished were the statues in the niches; those remaining in the early eighteenth century had been removed for fear they would fall on passers-by. The original design of the niche canopies seems also to have been simpli-fied.

This watercolour, probably exhibited at the Royal Academy in 1796 and later owned by a prominent Parliamentary official, depicts both the grandeur of the church and the charm of the contemporary scene. It shows how the Abbey, St Margaret's Church and the Houses of Parliament were knit together in a tight urban fabric, now swept away. All the houses depicted have been demolished.

36 a & b

Two Beasts from the Exterior
of the Henry VII Chapel

c. 1810–20
Combe Down Stone
(a) Dragon: 360 × 560 mm.
(b) Lion: 260 × 520 mm.
Dean and Chapter of Westminster

ills. 110, 111

Much of the success of the early nineteenth-cen-tury restoration of the Henry VII Chapel was due to the care with which the Master Mason, Thomas Gayfere, reproduced the mouldings of the orig-inal stonework and the decorative carving. A great number of sculptures, including these beasts, adorned the exterior of the Chapel and it would have been simpler—and cheaper—to remove them, in the same way that the decayed medieval sculpture had been treated during Wren's restoration. Such an approach had been acceptable to the Augustan age of the early eight-eenth century, with its pragmatic view of Gothic, but had ceased to be so to the Regency's more Romantic vision of Gothic. Gayfere taught his masons to carve these beasts with an authentic vigour, a quality which has been encouraged again in the present restoration.

110-111. Grotesque beasts from the Henry VII Chapel [36]

37

**Gable Cross
formerly on the South Transept**

c. 1872
Probably Chilmark Stone
1100 × 800 mm.
Dean and Chapter of Westminster

ill. 112

By the mid nineteenth century, the upper parts of the Abbey, restored a century before, were again much decayed. When Scott and his successor, Pearson, came to treat these areas, they could not bring themselves to replace features belonging to the Wren and Hawksmoor restorations, which they considered 'simply worthless architecture.' Instead, they devised new detailing in a thirteenth-century style based on their own profound knowledge of both English and European examples, which gradually changed the external appearance of the building.

The south front of the South Transept had been rebuilt on several occasions: in the mid fifteenth century, in the 1670s and again in 1814. Although the rose window retained its original thirteenth-century design, the gable above it was timber-framed to reduce weight on the wall, and the pinnacles were capped with ogee domes. In 1870–73 Scott rebuilt the gable in ashlar, decorating it with blind plate tracery and a figure of Christ, carved by Thomas Earp. He also reconstructed the buttresses and their pinnacles. The gable cross is a good example of Scott's archaeologically correct but bold style.

LITERATURE: Poole, 1889, pp. 220, 253–54, 284; Lethaby, 1925, pp. 85–87.

112. Gable cross formerly on the South Transept [**37**]

38

**Rood Cross designed for
the Confessor's Shrine
by John Thomas Micklethwaite**

1901–02
Gilded wood
1040 × 520 mm.
Dean and Chapter of Westminster

ill. 113

113. Rood cross designed by Micklethwaite [**38**]

This cross formed part of the reinstatement of a permanent altar and appropriate liturgical furnishings at the Shrine of St Edward, effected for the Coronation of Edward VII in 1902. The cross was placed upon the cornice of the Shrine, while a pall of velvet was thrown over the sixteenth-century wooden canopy. Even this modest gesture of Catholic symbolism shocked many members of the Chapter when first displayed. The cross, described by a contemporary as 'at the best only a moderately interesting piece of work,' was later coloured by Clement Skilbeck. It has recently been regilded and placed on the nave altar.

The designer of the cross was John Thomas Micklethwaite, successor to Pearson as Surveyor of the Abbey, who continued his predecessor's tradition of deep research into the history of the building. However, he was not in sympathy with the more refined aesthetic of men like Bodley and Comper. Some claimed that his 'sense of taste stood in inverse ratio to his vast archaeological learning' (Perkins, *Westminster Abbey*, Vol. 1, p. 112).

LITERATURE: Perkins, *Westminster Abbey*, Vol. 2, pp. 111–12; Perkins, 1960, pp. 40–42.

39

Cope made for the Coronation of Edward VII and designed by John Thomas Micklethwaite

1902
Crimson velvet with applied embroidery in gold thread
1550 × 1400 mm.
Dean and Chapter of Westminster

col. pls. XVIII, XIX

While Westminster Abbey was slow to follow the nineteenth-century return to medieval ritual and liturgical ornaments, by the time of the Coronation of Edward VII in 1902 it had accepted the need to change. As the Sacrist, Jocelyn Perkins, commented, 'the attainment of a lofty standard of worship and ceremonial…was felt on all sides to be imperative' (Perkins, *Westminster Abbey*, Vol. 2, p. 111). The set of seven copes of stamped crimson velvet, worked with crowned 'E's' and the keys of St Peter, were made by the celebrated firm of ecclesiastical embroiderers, Watts & Co., at a cost of £577. Their commissioning, like the adornment of the Shrine of St Edward (Cat. no. 38), was an early step on a path which led, during the next half century, to a transformation of the Abbey from being exceptionally ill-provided to possessing a rich array of furnishings. An inventory of 1948 lists almost as much in the Sacristy as that taken at the Dissolution four hundred years before (Perkins, *Westminster Abbey*, Vol. 3, p. 170).

LITERATURE: Perkins, 1960, pp. 37–38.

40

Processional Banner depicting the Virgin and Child flanked by St Peter and St Edward the Confessor designed by Sir Ninian Comper

1922
Embroidery on brocaded silk
1650 × 880 mm.
Dean and Chapter of Westminster

col. pl. XX

The restoration of a 'beauty of holiness' to the services and furnishings of the Abbey in the early twentieth century (see Cat. no. 39) is rightly associated with the name of the Reverend Jocelyn Perkins (1870–1962), Sacrist to the Abbey for over fifty years. Though never a member of the Chapter, he acquired great influence in the Abbey through his combination of a deep knowledge of English ecclesiology both before and after the Reformation with a keen discrimination in procuring the best materials available for new furnishings.

This banner, designed by Ninian Comper (1864–1960), was presented at Perkins' instigation by the Girls Friendly Society in 1922. It combines exquisite workmanship with the unashamedly sentimental Anglo-Catholic piety characteristic of the period. The Virgin and Child are surrounded by the patron saints of the Abbey and its heraldry. The reverse is embroidered with the cross and martlets of the Confessor.

LITERATURE: Perkins, 1960, pp. 118–21.

41 a & b

Ornamental Hinges: Design attributed to Sir George Gilbert Scott

c. 1870(?)
Metalwork
(a) 1000 × 810 mm.
(b) 930 × 730 mm.
Dean and Chapter of Westminster

ills. 114, 115

The original location of these hinges within the Abbey and their date have not yet been established; but they presumably belong to the High Victorian restorations of Scott and Pearson. It is the seriousness of these men's archaeological research even into details such as hinges that marks their Gothic work out from that of their predecessors. Whereas Hawksmoor, Keene or even Blore would have allowed the joiner to use contemporary door furnishings, architects after Pugin realized that a true medieval feeling required bold design such as these, based on ancient examples, for instance the doors at Stillingfleet in Yorkshire or Staplehurst in Kent.

114-115. Ornamental hinges **[41]**

42 a & b

Fragments of Choir Furnishings designed by Edward Blore

(a) Seat end from transept benches
(b) Door to pew
c. 1848
Oak
(a) 930 × 520 mm.
(b) 990 × 640 mm.
Dean and Chapter of Westminster

ills. 116, 117

The culminating work of Blore's surveyorship was his refurnishing of the choir in 1846–8, the 'greatest work which has been executed in the Abbey for generations,' according to Lord John Thynne, sub-Dean of the Abbey and principal promoter of the scheme (WAM 66416). The refurnishing was inspired on the one hand by an aesthetic distaste for the inadequacy of Keene's Gothic detailing of seventy years before and on the other hand by a practical desire for much more congregational seating. Blore designed two rows of sub-stalls in front of the canons' stalls and a third was squeezed in shortly after the inauguration of the choir. After considerable debate, it was decided that the choir should, for the first time, be opened into the transepts with no dividing screen or even grille. The two examples exhibited show the range of Blore's designs, from the richly detailed Gothic of the pew door—like the canopies and stall fronts, impeccably executed by Ruddles of Peterborough—to the bench end from the plain seating provided for the transepts. The bold functionalism of the latter seems fifty years or more ahead of its time.

LITERATURE: Perkins, *Westminster Abbey*, Vol. 1, pp. 153–83.

116-117. Choir furnishings designed by Blore [**42**]

118. View of the Choir, *c.* 1860, showing Blore's furnishings

119. Model of the propsed statue of Dean Stanley, by Joseph Edgar Boehm [43]

43

**Model for Seated Statue of
Dean Arthur Penrhyn Stanley
by Sir Joseph Edgar Boehm**

c. 1881
Coloured plaster
440 × 210 mm.
Dean and Chapter of Westminster

ill. 119

Dean Stanley was the outstanding personality of Victorian Westminster. His broad range of sympathy ran from Queen Victoria herself to the congregations of working class people whom he fervently encouraged to come to the Abbey. His churchmanship was equally broad, inviting un-

orthodox and even non-Anglican divines into the Abbey pulpit. Despite a passionate interest in the history of the building and the production of one of its classic texts, the *Historical Memorials of Westminster Abbey*, he was no ecclesiologist, nor a great enthusiast for architecture in itself.

This proposed memorial statue to him, presented to the Dean and Chapter by E. Baillie in 1956, shows Dean Stanley as both a social and a literary figure. By special royal permission, he was buried in the Henry VII Chapel, by the side of his equally distinguished wife: Lady Augusta Stanley, daughter of the Earl of Elgin. The monument as erected was a recumbent effigy, carved by Sir Joseph Edgar Boehm (1834–90) but designed by Pearson.

120. Monuments in Poets' Corner. Photograph taken before 1930

121. Design for Choir Pulpit by Blore [**44**]

44

Design for Choir Pulpit by Edward Blore: Elevation, Plan and Section

c. 1828
Pen and black ink
670 × 545 mm.
Trustees of the Victoria and Albert Museum
(no. 8741.117)

ill. 121

Though little appreciated today, Blore was one of the most eminent architects of the early Victorian period and enjoyed a particular reputation for the restoration of historic churches and houses.

By the time he was appointed Surveyor of the Abbey in 1827, the furnishings introduced into the Abbey during the eighteenth century were increasingly considered unworthy. The 'Whitehall' altarpiece had been dismantled in 1821 (see Cat. no. 20). Blore was commissioned to design two new items of furniture, more in keeping with the Gothic lines of the Abbey. One was an organ case, which seems to have been set to the west of that of 1728 and the other piece was a pulpit in the choir, to replace Keene's palm tree pulpit (see Cat. no. 29). The pulpit was constructed following this design in robust oak. Blore's cautiously archaeological but still two-dimensional Gothic design was soon considered out of date. Soon after his resignation as Surveyor, the pulpit was replaced by a new one designed by Scott. Blore's pulpit was given to Shoreham Church in Kent which, like that of Trottiscliffe, was in the gift of the Dean and Chapter. It survives in use, though alas cut down (*ill. 122*). Originally, it would have gained in effect by standing on a shaft 6 feet high, capped by this boldly carved corbel of a Green Man. The shield pencilled into a spandrel on the exhibited drawing presumably represents an idea for further embellishment which was never adopted.

LITERATURE: Perkins, *Westminster Abbey*, Vol. 3, pp. 38–39.

122. Pulpit by Blore now in Shoreham Church, Kent

45

Design for Pinnacle on the North Transept signed by Edward Blore

c. 1840
Pen and black ink
540 × 330 mm.
Trustees of the Victoria and Albert Museum
(no. 8741.116)

ill. 123

One of the most distinctive features of the Wren and Dickinson restoration of the North Transept was the erection of a tall pinnacle on the apex of the gable, matching those of medieval origin to either side. It is significant that, when it was severely decayed a century later, Blore was prepared to replace it with another. Unlike Scott and Pearson, he was not determined to redesign the whole according to a more accurate under-standing of medieval architecture, although he may have revised some of the detailing. It is also significant that the specification for the repairs was changed from Bath stone, such as had been used for the restoration of the Henry VII Chapel a few decades earlier, to Caen stone. Quarries were being opened in Normandy at around this time which offered, once again, this key material of many English medieval monuments at a very reasonable cost. Unfortunately, it proved inade-quate to resist London pollution and the rebuilt pinnacle had itself become severely decayed only thirty years later.

This drawing formed part of the bequest of Blore to the Victoria and Albert Museum. It in-cludes four corbel heads drawn rather crudely to represent king, bishop, monk and baron, some-what in the spirit of Walter Scott's novels.

LITERATURE: WAM 52203 A-C

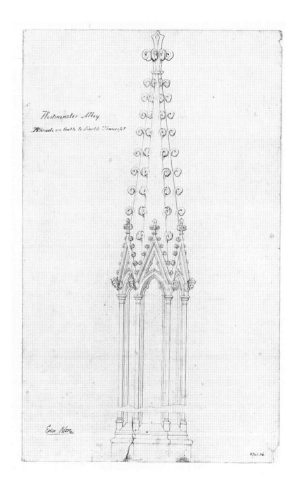

123. Design for pinnacle on North Transept by Blore [45]

46

**Model for the Restoration of
the Monument to Queen Philippa,
made by John Birnie Philip
and Samuel Cundy to the design
of George Gilbert Scott**

c. 1851
Alabaster and marble
1120 × 1400 mm.
Trustees of the Victoria and Albert Museum
(no. A15-1973)

ill. 124

The question of the restoration of the royal tombs
was much debated in the 1840s and 1850s. Both
national pride and the growing interest in the
authentic reproduction of medieval art made the
battered state of the Westminster monuments
appear intolerable. Shortly after his appointment
as Surveyor, Scott undertook a scholarly reconstruction of the tomb of Philippa of Hainault

(died 1369) which was translated into this full-
scale model by the skills of Samuel Cundy, the
Abbey Mason, and John Birnie Philip, one of the
finest and most prolific contemporary sculptors.
Although this model was shown at the Great
Exhibition of 1851 and three years later Parliament voted £4,500 towards the restoration of the
royal tombs, nothing structural was done. Instead, from 1857 onwards, Scott treated the
tombs with a particular concoction of shellac
which reintegrated their flaking stonework.

While Scott's design gives an accurate impres-
sion of the intricate detail and the colouring of the
monument as originally conceived, it remains a
High Victorian evocation of the Middle Ages.
The model was exhibited at the Great 1851 Exhi-
bition and at the Architectural Exhibition in 1852.
It has been housed since then at South
Kensington.

LITERATURE: Poole, 1889, p. 127; *Exhib. Cat.*, 'Victorian Church Art at the Victoria and Albert Museum,' London, 1971, Cat. No. F1, p. 56.

124. Model for the restoration of Queen Philippa's monument to the design of Scott [**46**]

47

Corbel with Two Lions for the Memorial Bust of Charles Kingsley by Thomas Woolner

1875–6
Granite
370 × 230 mm.
Dean and Chapter of Westminster

ill. 54

In the mid nineteenth century, there developed a trend in the Abbey to memorialize great men not by full-scale tombs but by busts. Five were erected in the south-west chapel (then the Baptistry) under Gibbs' great monument to James Craggs, creating, together with a statue of Wordsworth, a 'Little Poets' Corner'. They included Thomas Arnold, Dean Stanley's Head Master at Rugby and his life-long hero; Arnold's son Matthew, the writer; John Keble, the poet of the Oxford Movement; F. D. Maurice, the founder of Christian Socialism; and Charles Kingsley (1819–75), the writer of such famous novels as the *Water Babies* and *Westward Ho!* and also a canon of the Abbey. The monuments were all displaced in 1932 when a chapel was created there. (It was at first dedicated as the Chapel of the Holy Cross from 1932 to 1944, and then re-dedicated to St George).

The corbel by Thomas Woolner (1825–92) is characteristic of Victorian taste in its robust design and bold colour and in its choice of texts, 'Quit you like men, be strong,' and 'God is Love'. Kingsley was one of the proponents of the muscular Christianity, which inspired Victorian enterprise both at home and abroad.

48

Design for Nave Pulpit by George Gilbert Scott

c. 1862
Pen and brown ink
660 × 510 mm.
Trustees of the Victoria and Albert Museum (no. E2279-1911)

ill. 125

Scott soon replaced the pulpit erected by his predecessor, Edward Blore, in the choir (Cat. no. 44). In the nave, his more substantial pulpit of limestone and Derbyshire marble was not erected until 1862. The monumental scale of Scott's design contrasts with Blore's more two-dimensional approach, just as the material changed from wood to stone. A pulpit in this position was made necessary by the introduction, revolutionary for its day, of regular public worship and preaching in the nave in January 1858 under Dean Trench. Particularly popular were the evening services directed to working-class men. Already by 1902 the pulpit was considered out of date and out of place and was moved to St Anne's Cathedral, Belfast, being sent into exile like the three preceding pulpits in the choir by Keene, Blore and Scott himself.

This drawing, given to the Victoria & Albert Museum by Scott's son John Oldrid Scott, was presumably prepared by one of the clerks in Scott's office.

LITERATURE: Perkins, *Westminster Abbey*, Vol. 3, pp. 39–40.

125. Design for the nave pulpit by Scott [48]

49

Elevation and Section for the Restoration of the Central Portal of the North Transept by George Gilbert Scott

c. 1875
Pen and black ink
630 × 920 mm.
Trustees of the Victoria and Albert Museum
(no. E2276-1911)

ill. 126

Scott regarded the restoration of the North Front as his crowning achievement at the Abbey. In 1875, he wrote a passionate and ultimately successful plea to the Dean and Chapter that he should be allowed to use his research of over twenty-six years to transform the front from the 'worthless' condition to which Dickinson had reduced it, back to 'the most glorious work of its kind which the country contains.' (WAM, RCO Box 5: Letter of 2 June 1875). Scott was engaged in the reconstruction of the portals at the time of his death in 1878 and the work was completed by his son John Oldrid Scott (who gave this drawing to the museum). The restoration of the upper parts was, however, a separate enterprise under Scott's successor as Surveyor, John Loughborough Pearson, and the controversial treatment of the rose window and gable was the responsibility of Pearson, not Scott. Scott's design for the portals was based on his own meticulous research but some elements, such as the (never completed) programme of sculpture, were conjectural. On this drawing there are slight pencil notes referring to the intended figures on the jambs and to the twenty-three angels and forty-four carved spandrels(?) included in the contract.

LITERATURE: Lethaby, 1925, pp. 70–71.

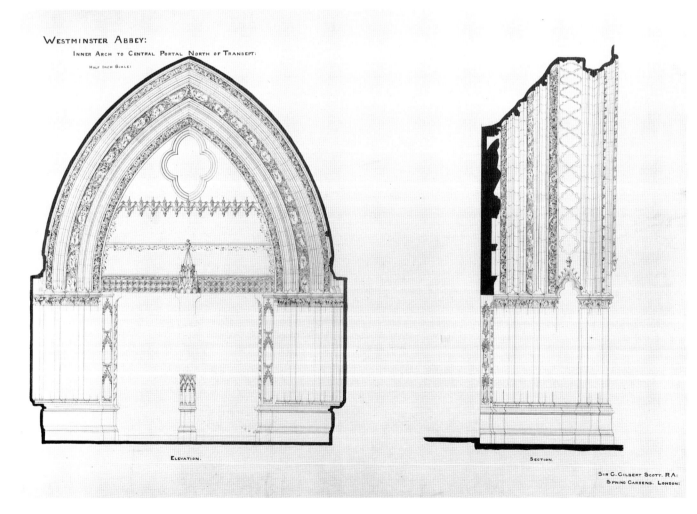

WESTMINSTER ABBEY:
INNER ARCH TO CENTRAL PORTAL NORTH OF TRANSEPT:
HALF INCH SCALE:

ELEVATION.

SECTION.

SIR C. GILBERT SCOTT. R A:
SPRING GARDENS. LONDON:

126. Design for the restoration of the central portal of the North Transept by Scott [49]

Bibliography

WAM: Westminster Abbey Muniments

Ackermann, R. and W. Combe, *The History of the Abbey Church of St Peter's Westminster*, 2 Vols, London, 1812

Ayloffe, J., 'An Account of some Ancient Monuments in Westminster Abbey', *Vetusta Monumenta*, II, 1789, pp. 1–15 (separate pagination for article)

Baker, M., 'Roubiliac's Argyll Monument and the Interpretation of Eighteenth-Century Sculptors' Designs,' *Burlington Magazine*, 134, 1992, pp. 785–97

Barlow, F., *The Life of King Edward*, revised edition, Oxford, 1992

Benton, T., 'Westminster Abbey and the Wren Office', in *A Gothic Symposium*, Georgian Group, 1983, no pagination

Binski, P., 'The Cosmati at Westminster and the English Court style', *The Art Bulletin*, LXXII, No. 1, 1990, pp. 6–34

Binski, P., *Westminster Abbey and the Plantagenets: Kingship and the representation of Power 1200-1400*, New Haven and London, 1995

Browne, P., *An Account and Description of the Cathedral Church of the Holy Trinity, Norwich, and its Precincts*, Norwich, 1807

Carpenter, E. F., ed., *A House of Kings*, London, 1966

Cocke, T., 'The Architectural History of Ely Cathedral from 1540–1840,' in *Medieval Art and Architecture at Ely Cathedral*, British Archaeological Association Conference Transactions for the year 1976, 1979, pp. 71–77

Cocke, T., 'James Essex,' in *The Architectural Outsiders*, ed. R. Brown, London, 1985, pp. 98–113

Cocke, T., and P. Kidson, *Salisbury Cathedral, Perspectives on the Architectural History*, Her Majesty's Stationery Office, 1993

Colvin, H. M., ed., *The History of the King's Works*, 6 Vols, London, 1963–82

Colvin, H. M., *A Biographical Dictionary of British Architects 1600–1840*, London, 1978

Cottingham, L. N., *Plans, Elevations, Sections and Details of King Henry VII's Chapel, Westminster*, 2 Vols, London, 1822–29

Cray, J., 'Paintings by Thornhill at Chinnor,' in *Burlington Magazine*, 132, 1990, pp. 789–93

Crull, J., *The Antiquities of St Peter's or the Abbey Church of Westminster*, 2 Vols, 3rd edn, London, 1722

Dart, J., *Westmonasteriensia, Or the History and Antiquities of the Abbey Church of St Peter's, Westminster*, 2 Vols, London, 1723

Ecclesiologist, IX, 1849, p. 334

Evelyn, J., *An Account of Architects and Architecture*, published as appendix to Evelyn's translation of *A Parallel of the Ancient Architecture with the Modern*, by S. de Freart, 4th edn, London, 1733

Field, J., *The King's Nurseries, the Story of Westminster School*, London, 1987

Foster, P., *Ten Years of Restoration at Westminster Abbey*, Ecclesiological Society, 1985

Gem, R. D. H., 'The Romanesque Rebuilding of Westminster Abbey', *Proceedings of the Battle Conference in Anglo-Norman Studies*, III, 1980, pp. 33–60

Gentleman's Magazine, 1, 1843

Green, D., 'A Lost Grinling Gibbons Masterpiece,' *Country Life*, 131, 1962, pp. 164–66

Gunn, S. J. and P. Lindley, eds., *Cardinal Wolsey: Church, State and Art*, Cambridge, 1991

Hacket, J., *Scrinia Reserata: A Memorial Offer'd to the Great Deservings of John Williams DD*, 2 Vols, London, 1692–93

Harvey, A. and R Mortimer, eds., *The Funeral Effigies of Westminster Abbey*, Woodbridge, 1994

Harvey, B., *Westminster Abbey and its Estates in the Middle Ages*, Oxford, 1977

Harvey, B., *Living and Dying in England 1100–1540, The Monastic Experience*, Oxford, 1993

Hooke, R., *The Diary of Robert Hooke, 1670–80*, eds. H. W. Robinson and W. Adams, London, 1935

Hunting, P., *Royal Westminster*, Catalogue to Royal Institute of Chartered Surveyors Centenary Exhibition, London, 1981

Hyland, A. D. C., 'Imperial Valhalla,' *Journal of Society of Architectural Historians*, XXI, 1962, pp. 129–39

Jordan, W. R., 'Sir George Gilbert Scott RA, Surveyor to Westminster Abbey 1849–1878', *Architectural History*, XXIII, 1980, pp. 60–85

Keepe, H., *Monumenta Westmonasteriensia: or a Historical Account of the Original, Increase and Present State of St Peter's, or the Abbey Church of Westminster*, London, 1683

Knowles, D., *The Religious Orders in England*, Vol. 3, *The Tudor Age*, Cambridge, 1979

Lethaby, W. R., *Westminster Abbey and the Kings' Craftsmen*, London, 1906

Lethaby, W. R., *Westminster Abbey Re-examined*, London, 1925

Lindley, P., 'Westminster and London: Sculptural Centres in the Thirteenth Century', in *Diskurse zur Geschichte der europäischen Bildhauerkunst*, eds. H. Beck and K. Hengeross, Frankfurt, 1994, pp. 240–41

Lockett, R., 'The Restoration of Lichfield Cathedral: James Wyatt to John Oldrid Scott', in *Medieval Archaeology and Architecture at Lichfield*, British Archaeological Association Conference Transactions for the year 1987, 1993, pp. 115–39

Markland, J. H., *Remarks on English Churches and on the Expediency of rendering Sepulchral Memorials Subservient to Pious and Christian Uses*, Oxford, 1843

McDowall, R. W., J. T. Smith and C. F. Stell, 'The Timber Roofs of the Collegiate Church of St Peter at Westminster', *Archaeologia*, 100, 1966, pp. 155–74

Morris, W., *Westminster Abbey*, Society for the Protection of Ancient Buildings 1900

Neale, J. and E. Brayley, *History and Antiquities of the Abbey Church of St Peter, Westminster*, 2 Vols, London, 1818

The New Bell's Cathedral Guides, 'Westminster Abbey', Contributions by C. Wilson, P. Tudor-Craig, J. Physick, R. Gem, London, 1986

O'Neilly, J. G. and L. E. Tanner, 'The Shrine of Edward the Confessor', *Archaeologia*, 100, 1966, pp. 129–54

Pepys, S., *The Diary of Samuel Pepys*, eds. R. Latham and W. Matthews, Vol. 1, London, 1970

Perkins, J., *Westminster Abbey, its Worship and Ornaments*, For Alcuin Club Collections, XXXIII, XXXIV, XXXVIII, 3 Vols, London, 1938–52

Perkins, J., *Sixty Years at Westminster Abbey*, London, 1960

Pevsner, N., *The Buildings of England: London Vol. I, The Cities of London and Westminster*, Harmondsworth, 1973

Pevsner, N. and P. Metcalf, *The Cathedrals of England: Southern England*, Harmondsworth, 1985

Poole, H., 'Annals of the Masonry, carried out by Henry Poole, Abbey Master Mason 1856–67,' in *Journal of the Proceedings of the Royal Institute of British Architects*, Vol. 6, 1889, pp. 113–16, 136, 169–72, 187–88, 218–20, 253–54, 281–82, 301–304

Prothero, R. E., *The Life and Correspondence of Arthur Penrhyn Stanley DD*, 2 Vols, London, 1893

Prothero, R. E., ed., *Letters and Verses of Arthur Penrhyn Stanley DD*, London, 1895

Quarrell, W. H. and M. Mare, trans. and eds., *London in 1710, From The Travels of Zacharias Conrad von Uffenbach*, London, 1934

Quiney, A., *John Loughborough Pearson*, New Haven and London, 1979

Rackham, R. B., 'Building at Westminster Abbey, from the Great Fire (1298) to the Great Plague (1348)', *Archaeological Journal*, LXVII, 1910, pp. 259–78

Robinson, J. Armitage, 'The Church of Edward the Confessor at Westminster', *Archaeologia*, LXII, 1910, pp. 81–100

Royal Commission appointed to inquire into the present want of space for monuments in Westminster, First Report, London, 1890

Royal Commission on the Historical Monuments of England, *An Inventory of the Historical Monuments in London. Vol. 1, Westminster Abbey*, London, 1924

Scott, G. G. et al., *Gleanings from Westminster Abbey'*, 2nd edn [enlarged], London, 1863

Scott, G. G., *Personal and Professional Recollections,* London 1879

Stanley, A. P., *Historical Memorials of Westminster'*, 2nd edn [revised], London, 1868

Tanner, L. E., *Unknown Westminster Abbey*, Harmondsworth, 1948

Tanner, L. E., *Recollections of a Westminster Antiquary*, 1969

Vivian-Neal, A. W., 'Sculptures by Grinling Gibbons and Quellin', *Proceedings of Somersetshire Archaeological and Natural History Society*, LXXXI, 1935, pp. 127–32

(Hibbert-)Ware, S., 'Observations on Vaults,' *Archaeologia*, XVII, 1814, pp. 40-84

(Hibbert-) Ware, S., 'Observations on the Origin of the principal Features of Decorative Architecture,' *Archaeologia*, XVIII, 1817, pp. 336–39

Westlake, H. F., *St Margaret's, Westminster*, London, 1940

Westlake, H. F., *Westminster Abbey, the Church, Convent, Cathedral and College of St Peter's Westminster*, 2 Vols, London, 1923

Widmore, R., *Enquiry into the time of the First Foundation of Westminster Abbey'*, London, 1743

Widmore, R., *History of the Church of St Peter, Westminster'*, London, 1751

Worsley, G., 'Drawn to a Find,' *Country Life*, 1993, pp. 100–101

Wren, S., ed., *Parentalia*, London, 1750; [reprinted by Gregg Press, Farnborough, 1965]

Wren Society, Volume 7: *The Royal Palaces of Winchester, Whitehall, Kensington and St James*, Oxford, 1930

The Lapidarium in the gallery

Chronology

DATE	MONARCH	WORK IN WESTMINSTER
604	Ethelbert, King of Kent	Legendary Foundation of first church by Bishop Mellitus and King Sebert
c. 1045–50	Edward the Confessor	Beginning of Romanesque church
1065 28 December	Edward the Confessor	Consecration of Romanesque church
1066 6 January	Harold II	Burial of the Confessor
25 December	William I	Coronation of William I
c. 1095	William II	Construction of Westminster Hall
1161	Henry II	Canonization of St Edward the Confessor
1220	Henry III	Foundation of the Lady Chapel
1245	Henry III	Beginning of the Gothic rebuilding
1269	Henry III	Translation of the Confessor's relics to a new shrine
1272	Edward I	Cessation of building after death of Henry III
1376	Edward III	Resumption of nave rebuilding under Abbot Litlyngton
1387	Richard II	Royal promise of £100 a year to the 'New Work'
c. 1440	Henry VI	Building of Henry V's Chantry
1441	Henry VI	Building of screen behind High Altar
c. 1467 onwards	Edward IV	Resumption of work on nave by Abbots Milling and Eastney: vaulting and roofing of nave, completion of great west window
1503	Henry VII	Foundation of the Henry VII Chapel
1500–28	Henry VII - Henry VIII	Raising of West Towers under Abbot Islip
1532	Henry VIII	Death of Abbot Islip
1536	Henry VIII	Dismantling of the Confessor's Shrine
1540 16 January	Henry VIII	Surrender of the monastery
17 December	Henry VIII	Foundation Charter as Cathedral of diocese of Westminster
1550 29 January	Edward VI	Abolition of See of Westminster: Westminster Abbey retained as co-cathedral for the diocese of London

DATE	MONARCH	WORK IN WESTMINSTER
1556		
27 September	Philip and Mary	Abolition of Dean and Chapter
20 November		Reconstitution of the monastery under Abbot Feckenham
1557	Philip and Mary	Reconstruction of the Shrine
1559		
10 July	Elizabeth I	Second surrender of the monastery
1560		
12 May	Elizabeth I	Foundation of Westminster Abbey as Collegiate Church of St Peter
c. **1605–30**	James I	Repair under Deans Neile and Williams
1642		
25 May	Charles 1	Last meeting of Chapter until 1660
1643	Charles I	Meeting of Westminster Assembly of Divines
1643–44	Charles I	Iconoclasm
1649	Interregnum	Establishment of College to run Abbey and School
1660		
5 July	Charles II	First meeting of restored Chapter
23 September	Charles II	Last service of Presbyterian Minister
1662	Charles II	Restoration work under Deans Earle and Dolben, fabric awarded a dividend of one fifteenth of Chapter receipts
1697	William III	Act of Parliament awarding Dean and Chapter a share of Coal Tax for restoration and completion of Abbey
1699	William III	Appointment of Christopher Wren as Surveyor
1706	Anne	Gift of former 'Whitehall' altarpiece
1723	George I	Completion of restoration of North Transept by William Dickinson
1735	George II	Restoration of West Front by Hawksmoor
1745	George II	Completion of Hawksmoor's West Towers by John James
1775	George III	Replacement of choir furnishings by Henry Keene
1803	George III	Fire over crossing
1807–22	George III	Restoration of the Henry VII Chapel by Thomas Gayfere under James Wyatt
1820–21	George IV	Removal of 'Whitehall' reredos
1824	George IV	Restoration of altar screen by Bernasconi
1827	George IV	Appointment of Blore as Surveyor
1833	William IV	Organ case installed by Blore and west face of screen altered
1845–48	Victoria	Reconstruction of choir by Blore
1849	Victoria	Appointment of Scott as Surveyor

DATE	MONARCH	WORK IN WESTMINSTER
1858	Victoria	Introduction of nave services
1863	Victoria	Appointment of Dean Stanley (installed 1864: died July 1881)
1866–72	Victoria	Restoration of Chapter House
1867–77	Victoria	Embellishment of altar screen
1878–81	Victoria	Restoration of north portals
1878	Victoria	Death of Scott and appointment of Pearson as Surveyor
1884–90	Victoria	Restoration of upper parts of North Transept by Pearson
1902	Edward VII	Coronation of Edward VII and rehabilitation of Shrine by Micklethwaite
1912–13	George V	Introduction of electricity to the Abbey
1930–35		Repairs by Tapper to the Henry VII Chapel
1939–45	George VI	World War II: bomb damage to lantern and the Henry VII Chapel
1952 onwards	Elizabeth II	Restoration of Abbey under Dykes Bower, Foster and Buttress

Seal of the Commonwealth period, showing the North Front of the Abbey

List of Abbots, Deans and Surveyors of Westminster Abbey

ABBOTS SINCE THE CONQUEST

1049–71(?)	Edwin
1071(?)–75(?)	Geoffrey of Jumièges
1076(?)–85	Vitalis of Bernay
1085–1117	Gilbert Crispin
1121–36(?)	Herbert
1138–57(?)	Gervase de Blois
1158(?)–73	Laurence of Durham
1175–90	Walter of Winchester
1191–1200	William Postard
1200–14	Ralph de Arundel alias Papillon
1214–22	William de Humez
1222–46	Richard de Berkyng
1246–58	Richard de Crokesley
1258	Philip de Lewisham
1258–83	Richard de Ware
1283–1307	Walter de Wenlock
1308–15	Richard de Kedyngton alias Sudbury
1315–33	William de Curtlyngton
1333–44	Thomas de Henle(y)
1344–49	Simon de Bircheston
1349–62	Simon de Langham
1362–86	Nicholas de Litlyngton
1386–1420	William de Colchester
1420–40	Richard Harweden
1440–62	Edmund Kyrton
1463–69	George Norwich
1469–74	Thomas Millyng
1474–98	John Esteney
1498–1500	George Fascet
1500–32	John Islip
1533–40	William Boston
——	——
1556–59	John Feckenham

DEANS

1540–49	William Benson (formerly Abbot Boston)
1549–53	Richard Cox
1553–56	Hugh Weston
——	——
1560–61	William Bill
1561–1601	Gabriel Goodman
1601–05	Lancelot Andrewes
1605–10	Richard Neile
1610–17	George Montaigne
1617–20	Robert Tounson
1620–44	John Williams
1644–51	Richard Steward (never installed)

— —		1845–56	William Buckland
1660–62	John Earle	1856–64	Richard Chenevix Trench
1662–83	John Dolben	1864–81	Arthur Penrhyn Stanley
1683–1713	Thomas Sprat	1881–1902	George Granville Bradley
1713–23	Francis Atterbury	1902–11	Joseph Armitage Robinson
1723–31	Samuel Bradford	1911–25	Herbert Edward Ryle
1731–56	Joseph Wilcocks	1925–37	William Foxley Norris
1756–68	Zachary Pearce	1938–46	Paul Fulcrand Delacour de Labilliere
1768–93	John Thomas		
1793–1802	Samuel Horsley	1946–59	Alan Campbell Don
1802–15	William Vincent	1959–74	Eric Symes Abbott
1816–42	John Ireland	1974–85	Edward Frederick Carpenter
1842–45	Thomas Turton	1986–	Michael Clement Otway Mayne
1845	Samuel Wilberforce		

SURVEYORS

1698–1723	Christopher Wren	1878–97	John Loughborough Pearson
1723–36	Nicholas Hawksmoor	1897–1906	John Thomas Micklethwaite
1736–46	John James	1906–28	William Richard Lethaby
1746–52	James Horne	1928–35	Walter Tapper
1752–76	Henry Keene	1935–51	Charles Peers
1776–1813	James Wyatt	1951–73	Stephen Dykes Bower
1813–27	Benjamin Dean Wyatt	1973–88	John Peter Foster
1827–49	Edward Blore	1988—	Donald Ronald Buttress
1849–78	George Gilbert Scott		

Angel holding a Sundial, from the North Transept, thirteenth century

Acknowledgements

The Dean and Chapter of Westminster wish to express their profound gratitude to those who made this exhibition possible by the loan of exhibits: the Vicar and Churchwardens of St Andrew's, Burnham-on-Sea; the Rector and Churchwardens of St Andrew's, Chinnor; the Trustees of the Victoria & Albert Museum; and private collectors.

Particular tribute should also be made to the devoted work of Thomas Cocke, who devised the exhibition, selected the exhibits and advised on all aspects of presentation.

Thanks are also due to Donald Buttress, the present Surveyor of the Fabric, who was responsible for all the displays in the Masons' Yard, contributed an account of the twentieth-century restorations, and assisted in the planning of the exhibition at every stage; to George Burroughs (Clerk of the Works), Richard Mortimer (Keeper of the Muniments) and Tony Platt (Honorary Keeper of the Lapidarium); to many others on the staff of the Abbey, especially Michael Carson, Maureen Jupp, Tony Rees, Christine Reynolds, Emma St John-Smith and Dr Tony Trowles; and to all who work and worship in St Margaret's Church for their tolerance of the disturbance caused by this exhibition.

The exhibition in St Margaret's Church was designed and installed by Stanton-Williams and tribute should be paid to the imagination and good humour of Paul Williams and Michael Langley. Graphics (including the catalogue cover) were by Crispin Rose-Innes Ltd. Security equipment was generously provided by 3DIS Ltd. and personnel by UniTrust Protection Services Ltd.

The displays in the Masons' Yard were generously supported by the Westminster Abbey Trust and arranged with the willing cooperation of Mowlem plc and the staff and workforce of Rattee and Kett.

The catalogue was written and edited by Thomas Cocke, who gratefully acknowledges comments on the text by Paul Binski, Howard Colvin, Peter Foster, Barbara Harvey, Phillip Lindley, John Physick and Tim Tatton-Brown but takes full responsibility for all errors that remain. Much help was received from Harvey Miller Publishers, and especially from Elly Miller, Jean-Claude Peissel and Lorena Casas.

Particular thanks are due to Dr Non Vaughan-Thomas for her unstinting work as Exhibition Coordinator and to Mandy Glass for patiently typing a complicated manuscript.

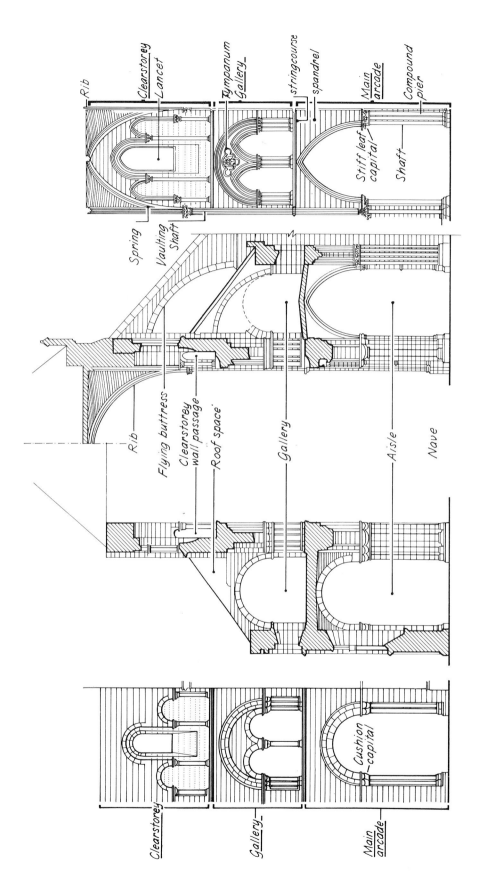

Diagrammatic explanation of architectural terms.

(Reproduced from *Recording a Church: an Illustrated Glossary* by Thomas Cocke, et al.
Drawing by George Wilson. Published by the Council for British Archaeology)

Rib
Clearstorey
Lancet
Tympanum
Gallery
stringcourse
spandrel
Main arcade
Compound pier
Stiff leaf capital
Shaft
Spring
Vaulting Shaft

Rib
Flying buttress
Clearstorey wall passage
Roof space
Gallery
Aisle
Nave

Clearstorey
Gallery
Main arcade
Cushion capital

Vault boss from the Muniment Room, thirteenth century